T4-ADP-001

STRAND PRICE
$5.00

52 REASONS TO VOTE FOR OBAMA

FORWARD.

52 REASONS TO VOTE FOR OBAMA

BERNARD WHITMAN

Velocity • MASCOT

New York

My Dear Lila,

Thanks for showing your mom with us... We couldn't get by without her! By the way, Obama loves chiropractic!! (Reason #53)

xoxoxo
Bern

Copyright ©2012, Bernard Whitman. All Rights Reserved.
No part of this publication may be reproduced, stored in
a retrieval system or transmitted in any form by any means,
whether electronic, mechanical, or photocopied, recorded
or otherwise without the permission in writing from the author.

Requests for permission to make copies of any
part of the work should be submitted online
to info@mascotbooks.com or mailed to:

Velocity • Mascot
560 Herndon Parkway #120
Herndon, VA 20170.

ISBN-10: 1-62086-097-X
ISBN-13: 978-1-62086-097-7
Library of Congress Cataloging in Publication data is pending.
CPSIA Code: PRR0712A

Artwork and interior design by Danny Moore

Printed in the United States of America

www.mascotbooks.com
www.velocity-books.com

To my mother and father, for your quiet wisdom and unwavering support throughout the years.

To my husband, for your enormous strength and the undying love I rely on more than you could ever know.

And to my son, for your extraordinary inspiration and the hope you give me each and every day.

ACKNOWLEDGMENTS

Like most things in life, this effort would not have been possible without the help and support of so many people.

I first would like to thank my husband, Scott Helfgott, who gave me the support and space I needed to write this book. As I always say, without you, none of this would be possible. I'd also like to thank my son, Zach, whose words of encouragement from the UK and Russia kept me going throughout the process. And I'd like to thank my sisters, Fran Ostendorf and Harriet Dunkerley, my folks, Nelson and Gerda Whitman and Esther Helfgott, and my many friends and family for their kind wishes and inspiration.

A special note of thanks goes to my incredible staff at Whitman Insight Strategies: Eric Bornstein, for pulling together much of the background research I relied on in writing the manuscript; our interns, Drew Primps and Amy Casale, who provided much needed support during the writing process; Scott Kotchko and Anastasia Saltarelli, who ran the show during my seclusion; and Marcelle Wolfe, my loyal assistant, who keeps everything moving forward.

I also want to thank my incredible team at Velocity Press and Mascot Books: Stan Pottinger, for all his guidance and support; Naren Aryal, for coordinating the effort; Danny Moore for his amazing illustrations; my editor, Rachel Burd, for her encouragement and direction; my fact checker, Jane Cavolina, for pushing me to source everything, and then making sure it was correct; and my copyeditor, Diane Aronson, for her exquisite attention to detail.

I especially want to thank the beautiful, still mostly undiscovered gem of Ocean Grove, New Jersey, where I wrote most of the book, and particularly to thank Bob and Marie Capozzi, for renting me part of their seaside home so I could write in quiet solitude, away from the hustle and bustle of New York. And many thanks to Erin Moran, for renting me her condo so I could finish the manuscript. A special shout-out goes to the Nespresso machine, which I coffee-napped from our office: I never could have done it without you.

I want to thank my trainer, Steve Kuchinsky, for getting my body in shape for this marathon, and I want to thank my teacher Moshe Rosenberg for first introducing me to the power of Kabbalah.

Finally, I want to give special acknowledgement to two dear friends and colleagues I have known for twenty years: Tom Cotton, who read every word of the initial manuscript and provided invaluable feedback and counsel; and Mike Berland, who gave me my start in this business more than two decades ago, and brought this project to me. I am extraordinarily grateful to you both.

TABLE OF CONTENTS

Acknowledgments vii

Introduction 1

1. Killing Osama bin Laden 5
2. Ending the War in Iraq: A Promise Kept 8
3. Twenty-eight Straight Months of Job Growth, Creating 4.4 Million New Private Sector Jobs 11
4. Delivered for the Middle Class 14
5. Cut Taxes for 160 Million Middle-Class Americans 18
6. Reformed Health Care 21
7. Cut Taxes and Provided Capital for Small Business 26
8. Prevented Another Great Depression 31
9. Saved the U.S. Auto Industry 35
10. The Freedom to Marry 37
11. Reformed Wall Street 40
12. Protected Women's Health 43
13. Transforming Our Schools and Making College More Affordable 46

14. Making the United States a Leader in Energy Production 49

15. Improving Veterans' Lives 52

16. Cut Unfair Credit Card Fees 55

17. Protected Medicare 57

18. The Stock Market 60

19. Responsible Immigration Reform 62

20. Commander in Chief for the Twenty-First Century 65

21. Keeping Our Homes 67

22. $1 Trillion in Spending Cuts 71

23. Equal Pay for Women 73

24. Supreme Court Appointments 75

25. Supports Science That's Helping Every American 78

26. Repeal of "Don't Ask, Don't Tell" 82

27. Mitt Romney 86

28. Kept His Campaign Promises 92

29. Forward versus Backward 94

30. A True Leader 98

31. Fuel Standards Doubling 101

32. Leadership in Afghanistan 104

33. Embodiment of the American Dream 107

34. Celebration and Advancement of Diversity 109

35. Nobel Peace Prize 112

36. Joe Biden 114

37. Hillary Clinton 117

38. Balance Against Congress 120

39. Michelle 123

40. The Dude Can Shoot Hoops 126

41. Malia and Sasha 130

42. The Guy Can Sing 133

43. His Huge Smile 135

44. He Drives the Right Crazy 138

45. Our Dogs Will Be Safe 140

46. My Barber Told Me To 142

47. I'm a Democrat 144

48. He's Cool 147

49. Second Terms Are Never Kind
       to Presidents (for My Republican Friends) 149

50. Republicans Will Have a Lock on Congress in 2014
       (Another One for the Republicans Among Us) 152

51. You Know Where He Stands 154

52. America Has Regained Its Global Prestige 158

Notes 163

52 REASONS TO VOTE FOR OBAMA

INTRODUCTION

Elections matter. We may like them, we may hate them. We may be sick and tired of campaigns, or we may look forward to the next one with the anticipation of a child. However you may feel, elections are important, and the choice we make will have dramatic impacts on the lives of hundreds of millions of people, sometimes immediately, sometimes not for a generation. Some of these effects are minute, hardly perceptible, while others are dramatic and far-reaching.

Americans took to the polls and elected Franklin Delano Roosevelt in 1932, and he pulled us out of the Great Depression. The election of 1960 brought us Kennedy, and later Johnson, and with that the promise of equality for black America. When Bill Clinton was elected in 1992 he helped usher in a wave of economic growth and prosperity unseen in modern times.

When we Americans go to the polls this November we will face as stark a choice as we have seen in generations: whether to go forward or roll dangerously backward; whether all Americans are truly created equal or whether the rights and privileges commonly associated with our great country will be reserved for a select and privileged few; whether we will continue to expand the American dream or whether we will see it contract into itself.

In a clear, concise, and easily digestible way I attempt in *52 Reasons to Vote for Obama* to outline why I believe Barack Obama should be returned to office. To be sure, a few of the reasons are tongue in cheek, meant to offer a bit of needed levity in an otherwise serious discussion of national priorities and fundamental principles. But the majority of reasons outlined herein represent what I see as an overwhelming rationale to cast a vote for the president, not only based on the extraordinary accomplishments he has achieved against considerable odds, but also taking into consideration what he is likely to build for this nation and the global community over the next four years.

The order of the reasons is not meant as an absolute ranking of importance, but rather should be considered in several groups, much like a play unfolds in three or four acts. The first half contains what I consider to be President Obama's greatest achievements, with the first ten being particularly noteworthy. Some of these, like the killing of Osama bin Laden and health care reform, are well-known; others, like cutting credit card fees and keeping nearly 75 percent of his campaign promises, are probably not. The second set begins exactly halfway through, with Mitt Romney as reason number 27. His position on the list is purposeful, for I believe Barack Obama should be considered first on his own merits, before his challenger is assessed. The reasons immediately following Mitt Romney cast this choice in sharper relief.

As with any long production, the audience deserves an intermission, and for that I provide a series of reasons meant to show a lighter side of Obama, as well as interject some humor and reveal a few of my own biases. After throwing in a few teasers for my Republican friends toward the end, I conclude with two broader themes, theses that speak first to what I see as fundamental character differences between the two candidates and finally to the larger importance of this election, one which will have profound implications not only for the citizens of our country, but for all of humanity.

52 Reasons to Vote for Obama paints a portrait of a president with an unrivaled command of the interconnectedness of issues, a true understanding of "the big picture," and an ability to rise above the fray to deliver powerful results for the American people. Barack Obama has displayed the strength of bold leadership akin to our greatest presidents, and with that has forever transformed the office. His daring, principled commitment has brought far-reaching change to America and the world, and I believe we are all better for it.

I hope you enjoy the book, no matter your political persuasion. For the Obama supporters out there, I hope I have provided some new information and energized you to spread the word to the masses. For those still on the fence, I hope I have given you cause to come over to our side. And for those of you committed to Romney, may this serve as a warning that you've got one tough battle ahead. And for everyone, regardless of party or ideology, please make sure to vote, and encourage others to do the same. It is not only a civic duty but a solemn responsibility that we must pass from one generation to the next. For those unable to vote in the United States, please share this message with those who can! This election is likely to be very close, and as we've seen before, every vote counts.

Finally, I encourage you to join in the conversation and share your own reasons by visiting 52ReasonsToVoteForObama.com. . . . I'd love to hear from you!

—Bernard Whitman
Ocean Grove, New Jersey
July 7, 2012

REASON 01

KILLING OSAMA BIN LADEN

Thanks to President Obama, bin Laden is dead and General Motors is alive. You have to ask yourself, if Gov. Romney had been president, could he have used the same slogan— in reverse?

—Vice President Joe Biden, April 26, 2012[1]

The killing of Osama bin Laden represents one of the most daring moments of Obama's presidency, or any presidency for that matter. The successful outcome of the raid was hardly certain, and the guts it took speak volumes about the kind of leader Barack Obama is. Defense Secretary Robert Gates was against the decision, as was General James Cartwright, vice chairman of the Joint Chiefs of Staff. Even Vice President Biden was against the assault. At the end of the day, Barack Obama and Barack Obama alone decided on sending in SEAL Team Six. Not an easy decision to be sure, but he made the right one.

George W. Bush's brash and bellicose Defense Secretary Donald Rumsfeld had called off a similar raid six years earlier, raising many of the same concerns that Obama administration officials said complicated the bin Laden mission. Rumsfeld decided the raid was too dangerous and might cause a rift with Pakistan (since they'd been such a reliable and trustworthy ally).

The bin Laden assault also underscores some core values and fundamental character strengths of Obama: keeping promises, trusting your instincts, and following through, even in the face of tremendous adversity. These are some of the true qualities America wants, deserves, and expects in its chief executive.

Almost four years before the raid, in August 2007, then senator Barack Obama pledged to kill bin Laden, first in a speech at the Woodrow Wilson Center and later during a Democratic primary debate:

> If we have actionable intelligence about high-value terrorist targets and President Musharraf won't act,
> we will. I think that if we have Osama bin Laden in
> our sights, and we've exhausted all other options,
> we should take him out before he plans to kill another
> 3,000 Americans. I think that's common sense.[2]

In a March 2008 speech in Fayetteville, North Carolina, Obama underscored his position, remarking, "If we have actionable intelligence about high-level al Qaeda targets in Pakistan's border region, we must act if Pakistan will not or cannot."[3]

And during an October 2007 debate with Senator John McCain, Obama stated unequivocally, "We will kill bin Laden. We will crush al Qaeda. That has to be our biggest national security priority."[4]

This approach stands in stark contrast to that of President Bush, who said just a few months after the 9/11 attacks:

> Who knows if he's hiding in some cave or not; we haven't heard from him in a long time. And the idea of focusing on one person is—really indicates to me people don't understand the scope of the mission. Terror is bigger than one person. And he's just—he's a person who's now been marginalized. . . . So I don't know where he is. You know, I just don't spend that much time on him, to be honest with you.[5]

Bin Laden was then allowed to escape from Tora Bora, after pleas from commanders and intelligence officials for more resources were rebuffed by top Bush national security officials.[6] In late 2005, the CIA shuttered its bin Laden unit entirely, as part of a broader shift of resources toward Iraq. And by 2006, as the war in Iraq was foundering, Bush told Fred Barnes of the *Weekly Standard* that capturing bin Laden was "not a top priority use of American resources."[7]

Apparently, when Mitt Romney ran for president last time around, he agreed, saying in April 2007 that killing Osama bin Laden was "insignificant" and concluding that it wasn't "worth moving Heaven and Earth."[8] Four months later, in August 2007, Romney blasted Barack Obama for vowing to strike al Qaeda targets inside Pakistan if necessary, saying, "I do not concur, in the words of Barack Obama, in a plan to enter an ally of ours."[9]

Good thing Obama was president last May, and not Bush or Romney.

REASON 02

ENDING THE WAR IN IRAQ: A PROMISE KEPT

ENDING THE WAR IN IRAQ

From the very beginning, Barack Obama was against the war in Iraq, a fact that few elected officials can claim. Even as an Illinois senator, Obama stated his clear opposition to the war in a speech to the Illinois state legislature in October 2002:

> I know that invasion of Iraq without a clear rationale and without strong international support will only fan the flames of the Middle East and encourage the worst rather than best impulses in the Arab world and strengthen the recruitment arm of al Qaeda. I am not opposed to all wars; I am opposed to dumb wars.[10]

In a July 14, 2008, op-ed in the *New York Times*, Obama firmly restated his opposition to the war, saying he considered it a "grave mistake" to have entered Iraq when it posed no imminent threat and had nothing to do with 9/11; the candidate vowed to end the war if elected president. He also emphasized the importance of a gradual and careful withdrawal during a sixteen-month period, hoping to get the last troops out during summer 2010, a timetable that even then prime minister al-Maliki of Iraq endorsed.

In his inaugural address, President Obama declared, "We will begin to responsibly leave Iraq to its people," and on his first full day in office, January 21, 2009, Obama ordered his national security team to conduct a comprehensive review of the situation in Iraq to determine the best, safest, and most efficient strategy for redeployment.[11] On February 27, 2009, Obama delivered his first speech on Iraq, one to a group of Marines at Camp Lejeune, in North Carolina, and he outlined a timeline that included combat in Iraq ending by August 2010 and full redeployment by the end of 2011, with a limited number of troops remaining in Iraq through 2011 to perform special missions, such as training Iraqi soldiers, protecting U.S. officials, and pursuing counterterrorism.[12]

True to his word, President Obama announced the end of combat missions in Iraq on August 31, 2010, stating, "Our commitment in Iraq is changing—from a military effort led by our troops to a civilian effort led by our diplomats." On October 21, 2011, Obama fulfilled his promise by announcing that all troops would be out of Iraq by the end of 2011, ending the eight-year war, and on December 18, 2011, the last U.S. troops left Iraq.[13]

- 4,487 U.S. troops killed
- 32,223 U.S. troops wounded
- More than 100,000 Iraqi civilians killed[14]
- Nearly 1.5 million U.S. troops served
- More than $1 trillion spent

President Obama would not have started the war in Iraq, but he certainly delivered on his promise to end it.

REASON 03

TWENTY-EIGHT STRAIGHT MONTHS OF JOB GROWTH, CREATING 4.4 MILLION NEW PRIVATE SECTOR JOBS

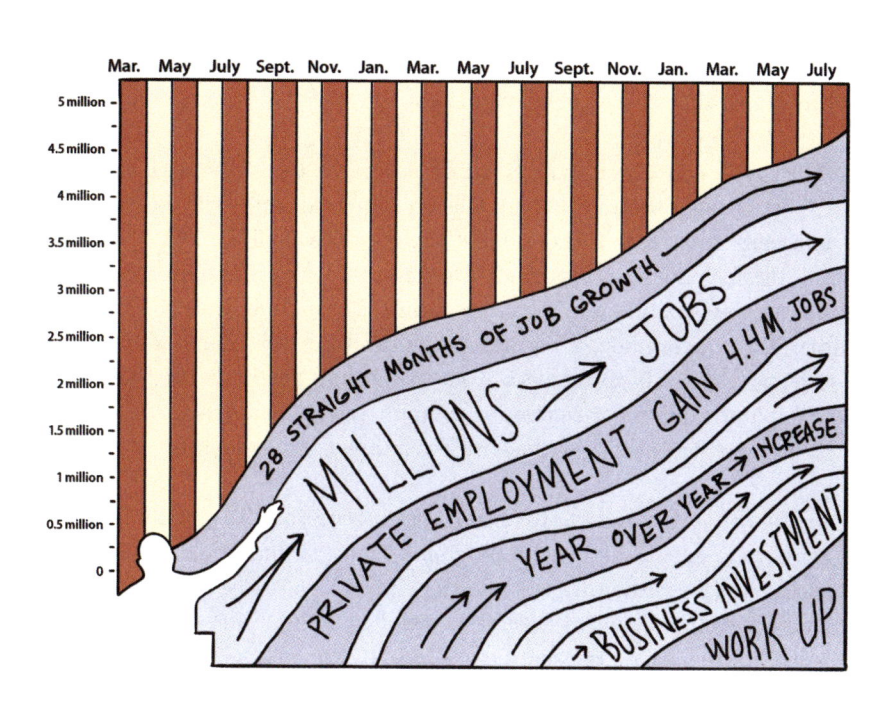

28 STRAIGHT MONTHS OF JOB GROWTH
MILLIONS → JOBS
PRIVATE EMPLOYMENT GAIN 4.4M JOBS
YEAR OVER YEAR → INCREASE
BUSINESS INVESTMENT
WORK UP

When President Obama took office, the economy was losing more than 700,000 jobs a month.[15] President Obama acted quickly to pass the American Recovery and Reinvestment Act, which cut taxes for small businesses and 95 percent of working families.[16] The law also included emergency funding to support about 300,000 educator jobs,[17] more than 4,600 law enforcement positions,[18] and investments in the clean energy sector that supported 224,500 jobs through 2010.

Since the end of 2009, business investment has grown at a rate of 18 percent, and exports have increased 32 percent, for a total of $2 trillion. The American manufacturing industry has added nearly 500,000 jobs in the past twenty-eight months—the strongest growth for any twenty-eight-month period since 1995. So far this year alone, the manufacturing sector has added 154,000 new jobs.[19] In 2011, for the second straight year, the number of manufacturing jobs in the United States increased, after declining every year since 1998.

"Outsourcer in Chief" Mitt Romney claims that his business experience will help him keep jobs on American soil, but his business practices have done just the opposite. In June 2012, the *Washington Post* reported, "During the nearly 15 years that Romney was actively involved in running Bain, a private equity firm that he founded, it owned companies that were pioneers in the practice of shipping work from the United States to overseas call centers and factories making computer components, according to filings with the Securities and Exchange Commission."[20]

President Obama wants to encourage "insourcing" by getting rid of tax deductions for shipping jobs overseas and offering new incentives for returning work to the United States. Big-name companies like General Electric, Ford, Caterpillar, and Intel already are looking to create more jobs at home rather than outsource them overseas. The administration is also pushing for a $2-billion-per-year tax credit to encourage manufacturers to invest in struggling communities:

> I don't want America to be a nation that's primarily known for financial speculation and racking up debt buying stuff from other nations. I want us to be known for making and selling products all over the world stamped with three proud words "Made in America." And we can make that happen.[21]

In the face of the deepest economic crisis since the Great Depression, Obama has created 4.4 million private sector jobs during the last twenty-eight months, including more than 800,000 in first four months of 2012, the greatest first-quarter gain since 2006. At the same time, the public sector has cut 607,000 jobs since Obama took office, a 2.7 percent decline.

In contrast, George W. Bush had the worst track record for job creation since the government began keeping records in 1939, with 4.4 million jobs lost during his last year in office alone.[22] But he did manage to put another 1,742,000 people on the government payroll![23]

Under Obama, 4.4 million new private sector jobs in twenty-eight months versus 4.4 million jobs *lost* under Bush in just one year . . . you do the math![24]

REASON 04

DELIVERED FOR THE MIDDLE CLASS

Middle Class

We see an America where a growing middle class is the beating heart of a growing economy. That's why I kept my campaign promise and gave a middle-class tax cut to 95 percent of working Americans. That's why we passed health insurance reform that stops insurance companies from jacking up your premiums at will or denying coverage because you get sick. That's why we passed financial reform that will end taxpayer-funded bailouts; reform that will stop credit card companies and mortgage lenders from taking advantage of taxpayers and consumers.

—*President Barack Obama,
Parma, Ohio, September 8, 2010*[25]

Barack Obama has delivered for the middle class in ten important ways:

1. Created 4.4 million new jobs, including more than 500,000 manufacturing jobs.[26]
2. Cut taxes by more than $1 trillion, including tax cuts for 160 million middle-class Americans.[27]
3. Provided free preventive care and ended preexisting conditions and lifetime caps.
4. Cut late fees on credit cards, saving consumers more than $5.5 billion a year.
5. Stabilized the stock market, allowing average 401(k) balances to grow every year for every age group and job tenure.[28]
6. Helped over one million homeowners keep their homes by lowering monthly mortgage payments.[29]
7. Higher fuel efficiency standards mean families will save thousands of dollars at the pump.[30]
8. Tripled the college tax credit to $10,000 and doubled the number of Pell grants.

9. Expanded job, education, and training opportunities for returning veterans.
10. Extended unemployment benefits to nearly three million people who had been cut off.[31]

To expand on this progress, President Obama wants to use money saved after troops leave Afghanistan to help strengthen the middle class. As the president summed it up during a May 2012 speech:

> I don't think we should prioritize things like more tax cuts for millionaires while cutting the kinds of investments that built a strong middle class. That's why I've called on Congress to take the money we're no longer spending at war, use half of it to pay down our debt, and use the other half to rebuild America.[32]

According to the National Economic Council, the most fortunate American households today are paying nearly the lowest federal income tax rate in fifty years.[33] These taxpayers benefit from loopholes, deductions, exemptions, and preferential rates. In 2008, the richest four hundred taxpayers, all of whom made over $110 million, paid an average income tax rate of only 18 percent. According to IRS data, more than twenty thousand households with over $1 million in income paid less than 15 percent in 2009.[34]

That's why President Obama supports the Buffett Rule, named after the famous billionaire investor Warren Buffett. This legislation would ensure that the wealthiest taxpayers—those who make more than $1 million a year—pay at least the same tax rate as middle-class families.

We need to continue to rebuild our economy, expand opportunity, and ensure that the next generation has more opportunities than we do. To accomplish these goals, we need everyone to pay their fair share. That's not just good economic sense, that's basic common sense.

While Mitt Romney focuses on cutting taxes for the wealthy and shipping jobs overseas, Barack Obama has consistently delivered for middle-class families. In a 2010 speech the president gave in Ohio, here's what he had to say about his plans:

> [I]f [families] work hard and meet their responsibilities, they can afford to raise their children, and send them to college, see a doctor when they get sick, retire with dignity and respect. That's what we Democrats believe in—a vibrant free market, but one that works for everybody. That's our vision. That's our vision for a stronger economy and a growing middle class.[35]

That's Barack Obama's vision for America.

REASON 05

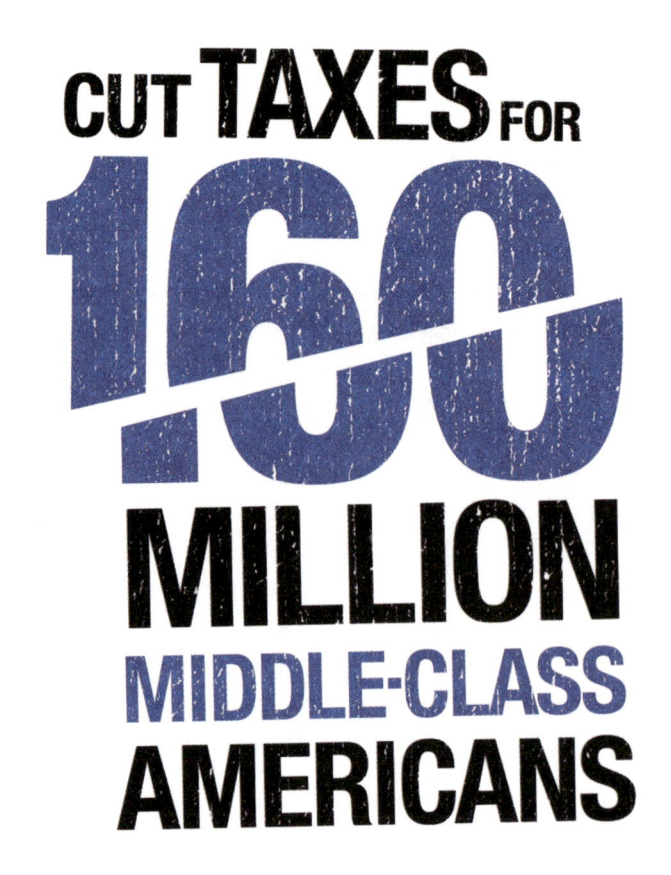

CUT TAXES FOR 160 MILLION MIDDLE-CLASS AMERICANS

CUT TAXES FOR 160 MILLION MIDDLE-CLASS AMERICANS

Less than one month after Barack Obama became president, he started cutting taxes for the middle class. And he hasn't stopped since. In fact, Obama has cut taxes far more than George W. Bush did during his first term. The total value of the Bush tax cuts were about $474 billion during his first four years. Obama's total? *More than $1 trillion,* and growing.[36]

Here's how it breaks down:

- The American Recovery and Reinvestment Act, aka the Stimulus, became law in February 2009 and included $282 billion in tax breaks, according to the White House:
    - Nearly all working families received a well-earned tax cut.[37]
    - Millions of families were lifted out of poverty by the tax cuts in the Recovery Act.
    - More than $150 billion in tax cuts helped low-income and vulnerable households.
    - About one million jobs were created or saved by these tax cuts alone.

- In December 2010, President Obama cut taxes for the middle class again:
    - Middle-class tax cuts were extended to prevent a typical working family from facing a tax increase of more than $2,000 on January 1, 2011.
    - A 2 percent payroll tax cut was provided to 160 million workers—giving the average working family an additional $1,000 tax cut.
    - The American Opportunity Tax Credit was continued, providing up to $10,000 for four years of college, helping more than nine million students and their families afford higher education.

- Expansions of the child tax credit and the earned income tax credit were extended, offering a tax cut for 15.7 million families and their 29.1 million children.

- This February, Obama cut taxes another $120 billion by extending the payroll tax cut to the end of the year, saving the typical working family about $40 a paycheck, or roughly $1,000 a year.[38]

In just two years, President Obama cut taxes more than George W. Bush did during his entire first term. And most of the Bush tax cuts were for the wealthy.[39] President Obama's tax cuts are focused where they are needed most—squarely on the middle class.

REASON 06

REFORMED HEALTH CARE

REFORMED HEALTH CARE

[T]oday, we are affirming that essential truth—a truth every generation is called to rediscover for itself—that we are not a nation that scales back its aspirations. We are not a nation that falls prey to doubt or mistrust. We don't fall prey to fear. We are not a nation that does what's easy. . . . We are a nation that faces its challenges and accepts its responsibilities. We are a nation that does what is hard. What is necessary. What is right. Here, in this country, we shape our own destiny. . . . That is what makes us the United States of America. . . . And we have now just enshrined . . . the core principle that everybody should have some basic security when it comes to their health care.

—President Barack Obama, at the signing of the Health Insurance Reform Bill, March 23, 2010[40]

Every president from Teddy Roosevelt to George W. Bush has tried and failed to fix the health care system. Americans spend about $2.7 trillion on health care every year, making up almost 18 percent of the U.S. economy,[41] and employing one in eight Americans. This is the fifth year in a row that health care costs will increase between 7 and 8 percent annually. The average yearly cost for a family of four under an employer plan has more than doubled in the last ten years, to $20,000. Last year, workers' out-of-pocket costs rose on average 9.2 percent to $3,280 for a four-person family. And if you aren't part of an employer-sponsored group you can plan on spending close to $7,120 out of your own pocket.[42]

The Affordable Care Act aims to bring health care costs under control and help more people get affordable health insurance coverage, including the fifty million who are uninsured today.

By requiring nearly all Americans to buy some form of health insurance beginning in 2014, health care costs will be spread to a larger group of individuals, thereby lowering costs. Without this individual mandate, along with measures to promote preventive care, health care costs will continue to skyrocket. And those with insurance will pay even more to cover the growing number of uninsured.

Most Americans support the individual elements of the health reform law, but many don't understand that without the individual coverage mandate, none of this would be possible.

So what are the benefits of health care reform?

An end to preexisting conditions

Insurance companies will no longer be able to refuse to renew or sell policies to individuals based on a previously existing condition. More than 13 million American non-elderly adults have been denied insurance for this reason, according to the Commonwealth Fund.[43] And insurers won't be able to discriminate based on condition or gender.

An end to annual or lifetime caps

Annual or lifetime dollar limits on coverage will be illegal. Previously, 105 million people were subject to these caps, and 20,000 were tossed out of the system every year. No more![44]

Prohibits insurance companies from dropping your coverage if you get sick

Before health care reform, companies could retroactively cancel an entire policy if any medical condition was not listed in the initial application—even if the condition was unrelated to that of the claim or the individual was not aware of it at the time. Coverage could also have been revoked for all the members of a family if even only one family member failed to disclose a medical condition.

Free preventive care

Last year, 86.5 million Americans with private coverage got at least one free preventive service, such as annual wellness visits, flu shots, mammograms, cervical cancer screenings, or bone density tests.

Americans under age twenty-six can stay on their parents' health plans

More than 2.5 million young people have already taken advantage of this benefit

Many small business owners are now getting tax credits to help lower the cost of health care

If you have up to twenty-five employees, pay average annual wages below $50,000, and provide health insurance, you may qualify for a small business tax credit of up to 35 percent (up to 25 percent for nonprofits) to offset the cost of your insurance.

Lower health care costs for seniors and people with disabilities

According to a June 25, 2012 report by the Center for Medicare and Medicaid Services, the average senior on Medicare will save $4,200 on their health care by 2021, and more than 5.2 million seniors and people with disabilities on Medicare have already saved $3.7 billion on prescription drugs, an average savings of over $700.

Coverage subsidies for low-income Americans

Out of this economic group—individuals making up to $44,000 a year and families of four making up to $88,000—nineteen million are expected to qualify.

Ability to buy private insurance through state exchanges

Beginning in 2014, families can save up to $2,300 on their health care each year and get insurance that isn't provided by or tied to an employer.

Unleash the entrepreneurial spirit

Americans won't have to stay in jobs just for the health coverage . . . they'll be free to start businesses, knowing they can get coverage on their own.

More information and greater transparency

Drug companies and medical-device manufacturers must report freebies they give to doctors; chain restaurants have to list calories under each menu item; insurance companies must provide a summary of benefits that is easily understandable, along with a glossary of terms.

Rebates to consumers if health insurance companies spend too much on overhead

Companies now must reveal how much they spend on health care versus administrative costs. If a company spends less than 80 percent of premiums on medical care it must rebate the amount that exceeds this limit. In 2012, nearly 12.8 million Americans will receive a total of more than $1.1 billion in rebates.[45]

Cuts the deficit by $210 billion over ten years (2012–21)[46]

This figure is the official estimate from the nonpartisan Congressional Budget Office and the Joint Committee on Taxation.

REASON 07

CUT TAXES AND PROVIDED CAPITAL FOR SMALL BUSINESS

[S]mall businesses produce most of the new jobs in this country. They are the anchors of our Main Streets. They are part of the promise of America—the idea that if you've got a dream and you're willing to work hard, you can succeed. That's what leads a worker to leave a job to become her own boss. That's what propels a basement inventor to sell a new product—or an amateur chef to open a restaurant. It's this promise that has drawn millions to our shores and made our economy the envy of the world.

—President Barack Obama, at the signing of the Small Business Jobs Act, September 27, 2010 [47]

President Barack Obama understands just how critical small businesses are to the American economy. That's why he's cut taxes for small businesses eighteen times since taking office. He's provided $200 billion in tax relief and incentives to American companies in the last three years to encourage new investment and job creation.

The Recovery Act, the Hiring Incentives to Restore Employment (HIRE) Act, and the Affordable Care Act included these tax breaks and credits, giving small businesses the boost they need to be more competitive and create jobs:

- A new small business health care tax credit
- A new tax credit for hiring unemployed workers
- Bonus depreciation tax incentives to support new investment
- Exclusion of small business capital gains
- Expansion of limits on small business expensing
- Five-year carryback of net operating losses

- Reduction of the built-in gains holding period to allow greater flexibility in investments
- Temporary estimated tax payment relief

The Small Business Jobs Act, the most significant piece of small business legislation in more than a decade, had eight specific tax cuts for small business, worth $12 billion:

- Zero capital gains taxes on key investments in small businesses
- The highest small business expensing limit ever—up to $500,000
- An extension of 50 percent bonus depreciation
- A new deduction for health care expenses for the self-employed
- Tax relief and simplification for cell phone deductions
- An increase in the deduction for entrepreneurs' start-up expenses
- A five-year carryback of general business credits
- Limitations on penalties for errors in tax reporting

Last February, Obama signed a law that allows businesses to expense 100 percent of certain investments, potentially generating more than $50 billion in additional expenditures to fuel job creation.

In November 2011, President Obama signed the VOW to Hire Heroes Act, providing tax credits up to $5,600 to businesses hiring unemployed veterans and up to $9,600 for those hiring veterans with service-connected disabilities.

This year President Obama is pushing Congress to pass more tax cuts to help two million small businesses hire workers and make new investments, discourage outsourcing, and encourage businesses to create jobs here at home. Obama's plan would give a 10 percent income tax credit to firms that create new jobs or increase wages in 2012. He also wants to extend 100 percent expensing so that firms can deduct the full value of certain investments through 2012.

According to the independent, nonpartisan Joint Committee on Taxation, the president's small business jobs and wages tax credit will provide more than $20 billion in direct tax relief targeted toward small businesses in 2012 and 2013, encouraging an additional $200 billion to $300 billion in new wages and jobs.

In addition to the eighteen tax cuts for small business, President Obama has made it easier for small businesses to gain access to the capital they desperately need. In just two years, according to the Small Business Administration, SBA, recovery loans have supported $30 billion in lending to more than 70,000 small businesses.[48] The Small Business Jobs Act provides more than $12 billion in additional lending support, with many of those loans going to rural or minority-, women-, or veteran-owned businesses.

The Small Business Jobs Act:

- Provides $30 billion in low-cost capital to community banks for small business loans.[49]
- Expands the number of small businesses eligible for SBA loans.
- More than doubles the maximum loan size for the largest SBA loans; increases the size of manufacturing loans; increases the size of SBA Express loans, which provide immediate access to working capital; and raises microloan limits, helping entrepreneurs and small business owners cover start-up costs.
- Enhances state small business programs, supporting at least $15 billion in additional small business lending, which encourages private-sector lenders to extend credit.

- Strengthens small businesses' ability to compete for and win federal contracts.
- Promotes small business exports.
- Expands training and counseling for small businesses.[50]

Through championing tax relief and more access to credit, President Obama has provided the essential fuel to help small businesses—the engine of our economy—expand and create jobs here in America, and drive our nation forward.

REASON 08

PREVENTED ANOTHER GREAT DEPRESSION

Let's not forget what was happening when Barack Obama entered the White House:

- In the twelve months prior to Obama's inauguration, 4.4 million jobs were lost, including 1.4 million jobs lost in the last two months alone of the Bush administration, according to the Bureau of Labor Statistics.[51]
    - That's nearly *23,000 jobs lost a day* during the closing two months of 2008.

- Our financial system was teetering on the verge of collapse.
    - Bear Stearns, Lehman Brothers, Countrywide, Merrill Lynch, AIG, Washington Mutual, and Wachovia collapsed or had to be rescued.

- Wall Street fell into a free fall.
    - The Dow plummeted 3,433 points, or 29 percent, in less than five months.

- The American auto industry was about to go under.
    - GM, Ford, and Chrysler were nearly bankrupt.

- Home foreclosures skyrocketed 225 percent in two years (2006–2008).
    - Foreclosure fillings hit three million in 2008.

- Fourth-quarter 2008 GDP sank by 8.9 percent.
    - This was the worst quarterly contraction since the Great Depression.

- American families' net worth was slashed by $11 trillion in one year (2008).[52]
    - That's right: $11 trillion. That's equal to the economic output of Germany, Japan, and the UK *combined*.

To prevent another Great Depression, Obama signed the American Recovery and Reinvestment Act less than a month after being sworn into office. Since then, we've seen eleven consecutive quarters of GDP growth, and twenty-eight straight months of private-sector job growth, for a total of 4.4 million new jobs over that period.

Princeton University's Alan Blinder and Moody's chief economist Mark Zandi estimate that without the financial interventions and the Recovery Act, we would have entered another depression—there would have been 8.5 million fewer jobs in 2010, and GDP would have been about 6.5 percent lower.[53] The nonpartisan Congressional Budget Office estimates that the Recovery Act saved as many as 3.5 million jobs.

Tax cuts represented the single largest element of the stimulus plan, and 95 percent of working Americans saw their taxes go down. The second-largest portion of the stimulus, just under a third, was funding that helped state governments avoid laying off teachers, firefighters, and police officers; prevented states' budget gaps from growing wider; and delivered critical relief through extended unemployment insurance, health coverage, and food assistance to those hit hardest by the recession.

The smallest element of the Recovery Act focused on rebuilding America's infrastructure, including the greatest investment in roads since the creation of the Interstate Highway System; construction projects at military bases, ports, bridges, and tunnels; Superfund cleanups that were long overdue; improvement in aging rural water systems; upgrades to outdated mass transit and rail systems; and more.

To strengthen our financial system, hold Wall Street accountable, and prevent the kind of financial meltdown that crippled the economy in 2008, President Obama signed the Dodd-Frank Wall Street Reform and Consumer Protection Act in 2010 that represented the toughest financial overhaul since the Great Depression.

To prevent the collapse of the auto industry, Obama extended emergency loans to GM and Chrysler. GM is now seeing record profits. The auto industry has added 230,000 jobs—the most in a decade—and GM and Chrysler have repaid their federal government loans.[54]

By Q3 2009, the economy was growing at a 2 percent rate instead of declining at a 9 percent rate as it had been previously.

"So in a remarkably short period of time, we were able to not just prevent a second Great Depression, but also to begin laying a stronger foundation" for growth, Treasury Secretary Timothy Geithner said in May 2012.[55] As a result, the economy is more productive now than before the crisis, with significant gains in investment and exports. In fact, corporate profits are now at record highs, well above precrisis levels.

President Obama had to dig out from the greatest economic downturn facing any president since FDR, while simultaneously fighting two wars. At least Roosevelt had nearly nine years under his belt before having to serve as a wartime commander in chief.

REASON 09

SAVED THE U.S. AUTO INDUSTRY

"**L**et Detroit go bankrupt," wrote Mitt Romney in a November 2008 op-ed in the *New York Times*:

> If General Motors, Ford and Chrysler get the bailout that their chief executives asked for yesterday, you can kiss the American automotive industry goodbye. It won't go overnight, but its demise will be virtually *guaranteed*.[56]

Mitt Romney could not have been more wrong.

Let's look at the facts:

- More than 1.4 million jobs saved[57]
- Nearly $97 billion in personal income losses prevented[58]
- More than 230,000 jobs added since June 2009, the most in a decade[59]
- Another 167,000 jobs are expected to be added by 2015[60]
- GM and Chrysler have repaid their federal government loans

The big three automakers—GM, Ford, and Chrysler—are profitable for the first time in seven years. GM recorded its highest profits ever in 2011, earning $9.19 billion, the most in its 103-year history. And GM regained its position as the world's number one automaker, with 2011 sales climbing in every region on the planet. GM sold more than nine million cars last year worldwide, up 7.6 percent. GM growth in the United States was even stronger, up 14 percent, while U.S. sales for Chrysler were up 26 percent from 2010.

The auto bailout was "one of the most successful things that was done during the economic downturn," remarked Kristi Dziczek, an economist at the Center for Automotive Research. If Mitt Romney had gotten his wish and GM and Chrysler had gone out of business, at least one million more jobs would have been lost, the federal government would have had to spend $14.5 billion to take over the two companies' pension plans, and federal spending on unemployment benefits for just the 129,500 workers at those two companies would have been staggering.[61]

Note to Mitt: Given that almost one in four workers in Michigan is supported by the auto industry, and more than 850,000 jobs in Ohio depend on the auto sector, you might want to flip-flop on this issue too.

REASON 10

THE FREEDOM TO MARRY

THE FREEDOM TO MARRY

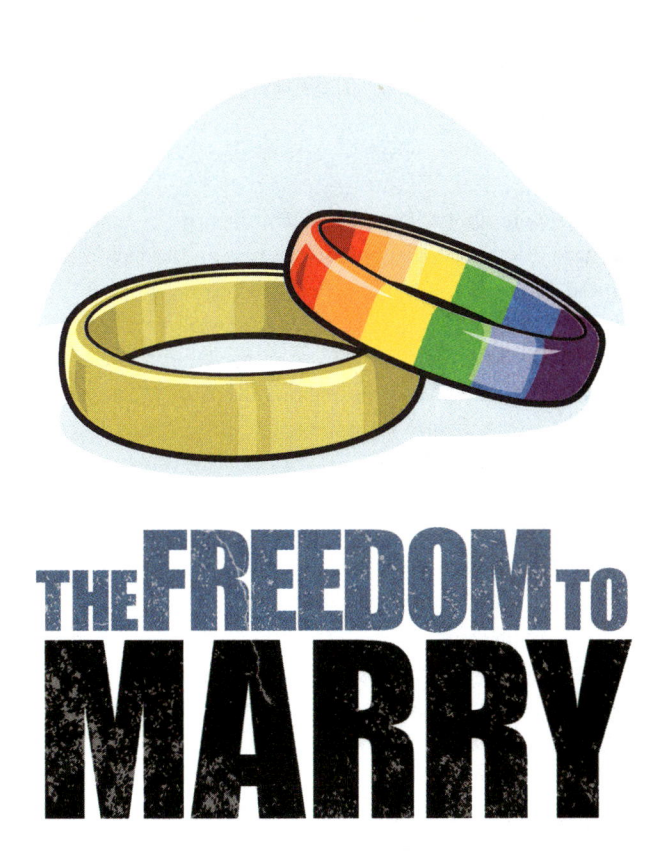

I have to tell you that over the course of several years as I have talked to friends and family and neighbors, when I think about members of my own staff who are in incredibly committed monogamous relationships, same-sex relationships, who are raising kids together; when I think about those soldiers or airmen or marines or sailors who are out there fighting on my behalf and yet feel constrained, even now that 'don't ask, don't tell' is gone, because they are not able to commit themselves in a marriage, at a certain point I've just concluded that for me personally it is important for me to go ahead and affirm that I think same-sex couples should be able to get married.

—**President Barack Obama, in an interview with Robin Roberts on ABC News, May 9, 2012**[62]

Marriage is about love, commitment, and family, universal truths and values that cut across political and ideological lines and should be accepted by everyone. The president's endorsement of the freedom to marry for gays and lesbians is an extraordinary step forward for everyone who honors the American traditions of equality, compassion, limited government, and equal rights. His journey mirrors that of tens of millions of Americans during recent years, as we now see people of all faiths, socioeconomic backgrounds, and political ideologies support marriage equality in record numbers. President Obama's support for the freedom to marry is a significant milestone, not only for the LGBT community, but for all Americans.

Polling shows significant support for Obama's stance on marriage. According to Gallup, 51 percent approve of the president's position, including 53 percent of independents polled.[63] In fact, at least a dozen national polls during the last two years show a majority support for the freedom to marry, with approval ranging from 50 to 54 percent.[64]

African Americans are now more likely than the general population to support the freedom to marry, with 59 percent saying they want to legalize same-sex marriage and 65 percent favoring Obama's position. Overall, strong support for the freedom to marry now overpowers strong opposition for first time (39 versus 32 percent). Opposition to same-sex marriage is at an all-time low, with only 39 percent saying it should be illegal.[65]

Even conservative Republicans are beginning to realize that marriage equality is inevitable. In a May 2012 memo, George W. Bush's pollster Jan van Lohuizen writes:

> Support for same sex marriage has been growing and in the last few years support has grown at an accelerated rate with no sign of slowing down. . . . The increase in support is taking place among all partisan groups. While more Democrats support gay marriage than Republicans, support levels among Republicans are increasing over time. The same is true of age: younger people support same sex marriage more often than older people, but the trends show that all age groups are rethinking their position.[66]

The tide is indeed turning toward equality, and Barack Obama's acknowledgment of support for the freedom to marry represents another major step forward in America's recognition that all people— gay and straight—are created equal, and deserve the same opportunities to live, to love, and to laugh, growing old together.

REASON 11

REFORMED WALL STREET

REFORMED WALL STREET

In the end, our financial system only works—our market is only free—when there are clear rules and basic safeguards that prevent abuse, that check excess, that ensure that it is more profitable to play by the rules than to game the system.

—President Barack Obama, July 21, 2010 [67]

In the wake of the economic collapse of 2008, Barack Obama was determined to hold Wall Street accountable. He worked to put into place reforms that would protect consumers and ensure such a crisis did not happen again.

The Dodd-Frank Wall Street Reform and Consumer Protection Act, the most comprehensive financial reform since the Great Depression, empowers consumers to make better, more informed financial decisions, ends taxpayer bailouts, and shines a light on the shadowy deals that caused the financial crisis.

Key Benefits[68]

I. The act holds Wall Street accountable:

- Ensuring no more bailouts.
- Preventing firms from being "too big to fail" by limiting the growth of the largest ones and restricting risky activities.
- Making sure that taxpayers will never again have to bear the costs of Wall Street's irresponsibility.

II. The act protects Americans from unfair, abusive financial practices:

- The Consumer Financial Protection Bureau will establish and enforce clear and consistent rules for the marketplace for families who want to buy a home, apply for credit cards, or are caught by unexpected bank overdraft fees.

III. The act closes gaps in our financial system:
- There will be greater transparency, more accountability, stronger capital buffers, and less concentration of risk among large financial firms.
- Banks will be prohibited from gambling with depositors' money (the Volcker Rule).[69]
- More power will be ceded to the Federal Reserve but with additional congressional oversight.
- Risky derivatives will be regulated and hedge fund trades will be brought to light.
- There will be oversight for credit-rating agencies and increased supervision of insurance companies.

As President Barack Obama remarked on the passage of Wall Street reform:

> The American people will never again be asked to foot the bill for Wall Street's mistakes. There will be no more taxpayer-funded bailouts—period. If a large financial institution should ever fail, this reform gives us the ability to wind it down without endangering the broader economy. And there will be new rules to end the perception that any firm is "too big to fail."[70]

Greater oversight on Wall Street means greater security on Main Street . . . a fact you can bank on.

REASON 12

PROTECTED WOMEN'S HEALTH

PROTECTED WOMEN'S HEALTH

For some strange reason, the Republicans have decided that a path to victory includes an unbridled assault on women's health. Just look at the uproar when the administration announced plans to require insurance companies to cover contraception. The Republican response? Hold a congressional hearing about birth control and invite five middle-aged men. No Women Allowed!

President Obama is determined to end that attack.

Before health care reform, women were much more vulnerable than men to high health care costs. Before health care reform, *simply being a woman was considered a preexisting condition.* Insurance companies would regularly charge women nearly double for coverage, even when maternity care was not included. Since women tend to use the health care system more, then they should be charged more, right? Wrong! This discrimination extended to the workplace, where businesses were charged more for covering women. Small businesses were especially vulnerable, and opportunities for women across the country may have been restricted.

Starting this summer, most insurance plans will be required to fully cover birth control without co-pays or deductibles as part of women's preventive care. This step will help more women make health care decisions based on what's best for them—not their insurance company—and could save them hundreds of dollars every year.

Under the new provisions in the Affordable Care Act, women will have access to the care and family planning services they need, saving some women up to $600 annually, or about $18,000 during the course of a lifetime. More than 50 percent of women eighteen to thirty-four say they've struggled to afford birth control.[71]

Providing contraception coverage will also save employers money. The National Business Group on Health estimated that employers would pay 15 to 17 percent more not to provide coverage than they would to provide it, after accounting for both the direct medical costs of potentially unintended and unhealthy pregnancy and indirect costs such as employee absence and reduced productivity.[72]

A majority of women have delayed seeking medical care due to cost, and one-third of women report forgoing basic necessities to pay for health care.[73] But under the health care law, insurance companies must provide free preventive services such as mammograms, Pap smears, and well-baby care. More than 45 million women have already taken advantage of these services. Current planning is for the addition in August 2012 of more services, including gestational diabetes screening and breastfeeding support, to the list of preventive care that must be covered without charge. By 2014, all new insurance plans will be required to cover maternity care.

Women now no longer need a referral to see their obstetrician-gynecologist, and they get to choose their primary care physician and their child's pediatrician from their plan's list of participating providers. The law also bans the outrageous practice of denying coverage to women who have had a Cesarean section or have been victims of domestic violence.

Thanks to health care reform, women have more control over their health care decisions, their lives, and their future. It's about time.

REASON 13

TRANSFORMING OUR SCHOOLS AND MAKING COLLEGE MORE AFFORDABLE

We will provide the support necessary for you to complete college and meet a new goal: by 2020, America will once again have the highest proportion of college graduates in the world.

—President Barack Obama, speaking at the University of North Carolina, February 24, 2009 [74]

Students need more financial relief than ever as student debt in the United States passed the $1 trillion mark in early May of 2012. Barack Obama gets it . . . he and Michelle just paid off their student loans a few years before moving into the White House! As the president remarked in April of this year:

> Check this out, all right. I'm the president of the United States. We only finished paying off our student loans off about eight years ago. That wasn't that long ago. And that wasn't easy—especially because when we had Malia and Sasha, we're supposed to be saving up for their college educations, and we're still paying off our college educations.

Here's how President Obama is making it easier for students to afford college:[75, 76]

- Pell grants have been doubled, helping eight million college and vocational school students across the country.
- Loans are delivered directly to the students who need them, rather than through a system that subsidizes banks, channeling more money to students.
- Income-based repayment options have been expanded for borrowers with high debt.
- There are increased investments in America's community colleges as well as in historically black colleges and universities, Hispanic-serving institutions, tribal colleges and universities, and other minority-serving institutions.
- It's easier to apply for college financial aid because of a simpler federal student-aid application.
- The largest college federal-tax credit has been tripled to provide up to $10,000 in tax credits for four years of college.

To ensure our young people are properly prepared for college, the president is helping to transform elementary and high schools across the country in many ways:

- Reforming No Child Left Behind[77]
    - States gain greater flexibility to focus more on learning and less on just testing.
    - Creative solutions are fostered, ones tailored to the local community.
- Encouraging reform through competition: Race to the Top:
    - States now vie for federal funding by putting forward their best plans for education reform.
    - Twenty-two states and the District of Columbia have won grants for boosting college and career readiness, developing data systems to track students, recruiting and rewarding good teachers and principals, and turning around struggling schools.[78]
    - Thirty states have changed their policies to become more competitive.[79]
    - It rewards entrepreneurialism and innovation in education.
- Advocating for merit pay to reward the best, most effective teachers
- Focusing on 5,000 of the truly failing schools and firing unqualified teachers and principals
- Expanding successful charter schools

Better schools + More college grads = A smarter, happier, more productive nation!

REASON 14

MAKING THE UNITED STATES A LEADER IN ENERGY PRODUCTION

ENERGY PRODUCTION

Despite what you may hear from the right, the Obama administration's record on energy is extraordinary. United States oil production is at an eight-year high, natural gas production is at an all-time high, and renewable energy production is up 27 percent.

Here are the facts:

- The United States now has more oil rigs (1,994) than any other country in the world, by far.[80]
- In 2011, less than half the petroleum consumed by the United States (45 percent) was imported from foreign countries, the lowest level since 1995.[81]
- By the end of 2013, the United States is expected to surpass Saudi Arabia and Russia in oil and gas production.[82]
- Natural gas production has regained its edge under Obama, leading to all-time highs, and this growth is projected to create more than 500,000 jobs by the end of this decade.[83, 45]
- Since 2009, President Obama has approved twenty-nine onshore renewable energy projects, including sixteen solar, five wind, and eight geothermal projects. By the end of this year, the administration will issue permits for enough renewable power from our public lands and our offshore waters to power three million additional homes.[84]
- Obama authorized the first nuclear reactors to be built in the United States in three decades, creating thousands of jobs and cutting carbon pollution by sixteen million tons each year compared to a similar coal plan, the equivalent of taking 3.5 million cars off the road.[85]

Since President Obama took office, America's dependence on foreign oil has decreased every year. In 2010, the United States imported less than half of all the oil it consumed—a first in thirteen years. In fact, net imports as a share of total consumption declined from 57 percent in 2008 to 45 percent in 2011—the lowest level in sixteen years. In the last year alone, we have cut net oil imports by 10 percent—a million barrels per day. Domestic oil and natural gas production have increased every year President Obama has been in office.

Thanks to the largest investment in clean energy in American history, the United States has nearly doubled renewable energy generation from wind, solar, and geothermal sources since 2008. Last year, the United States regained its title as the world's leading investor in clean energy technologies, beating countries such as China, India, and Germany.[86]

In addition, President Obama has repeatedly called on Congress to eliminate the unnecessary and wasteful tax breaks for the oil and gas industry, which would save American taxpayers $4 billion per year.

Smart leadership . . . Forward-thinking strategies . . . Integrated innovation.

REASON 15

IMPROVING VETERANS' LIVES

IMPROVING VETERANS' LIVES

You came home and sometimes were denigrated when you should have been celebrated. It was a national shame, a disgrace that should have never happened. That's why here today, we resolve that it will not happen again.

—President Barack Obama, on the treatment of Vietnam Vets, Memorial Day 2012[87]

President Obama is committed to protecting our veterans at home, just as they have protected us abroad. He has enacted a comprehensive and far-reaching package of reforms to protect military families and ensure they get the treatment, support, and honor they deserve.

Here are some highlights:

- The VOW to Hire Heroes Act provides tax credits for hiring veterans, expands education and training opportunities for vets, and offers disabled veterans additional vocational rehabilitation.

- An expansion of the Post-9/11 GI Bill makes it easier for National Guard and reserve members to qualify, provides a $1,000-per-year book allowance for active-duty service members and their spouses, offers distance-learning students a living stipend, and covers vocational training. In 2012, more than 500,000 participants are expected to receive almost $8.5 billion in tuition, fees, housing, and stipend benefits.[88]

- It is now easier for men and women who served in the armed forces to receive benefits for PTSD (post-traumatic stress disorder).

- Better and faster care for our veterans will be supported through integrating medical records into a unified computerized system to help prevent delays, lost records, and bureaucratic roadblocks, ending a backlog of 800,000 disability claims that could take six months or more to process.

- Enhanced care for veterans will be achieved through using hospitals outside of VA network, eliminating co-payments for catastrophically disabled veterans, increasing housing and transportation assistance for veterans living far from care facilities, creating a child care program for veterans receiving intensive medical care, and expanding support for homeless veterans.

- Extended assistance will be given to caregivers of

veterans, including specialized training, counseling, and health insurance.

- Homelessness among veterans has been cut by 56 percent. President Obama is first person in history to receive the Jerald Washington Memorial Founders' Award, the highest award in homeless-veteran advocacy, twice—a true indicator of the president's commitment to veterans. The initiatives outlined in the United States Interagency Council on Homelessness's *Opening Doors: Federal Strategic Plan to Prevent and End Homelessness* aim to end chronic homelessness by 2015, with a particular focus on ensuring our country's defenders have a place to call home.[89]

As the first president from the post-Vietnam generation, Obama is also determined to show our Vietnam veterans the appreciation and support they often didn't get upon their return home. Organizers of this effort are planning tens of thousands of commemoration events across the country, beginning in 2014. Obama wants to kick off the celebration, underscoring how the country has changed since Vietnam.[90]

We owe our veterans—who risk their lives every day to keep us safe—nothing less.

REASON 16

CUT UNFAIR CREDIT CARD FEES

Nearly 80 percent of American families have a credit card, and 44 percent of families carry a balance each month, according to the U.S. Treasury Department. Before Obama took office, Americans had paid an average of nearly $15 billion in penalty fees. Credit card debt has grown by 25 percent in the last decade, with delinquency rates up by more than one-third since 2006.[91]

To protect consumers and combat unfair rate increases and hidden fees, Obama signed the Credit Card Accountability, Responsibility, and Disclosure (CARD) Act shortly after taking office.

The Benefits:

- Bans unfair and retroactive rate increases
- Prevents unfair fee traps
- Plain sight/plain language disclosures
- Protections for students and young people[92]

In just one year, interest-rate hikes on existing accounts *fell by more than 87 percent*. The amount of late fees paid by consumers dropped by more than half, saving consumers *more than $5.5 billion dollars a year*. And over-limit fees have been virtually *eliminated*.[93]

What's in your wallet . . . a lot more cash!

REASON 17

PROTECTED MEDICARE

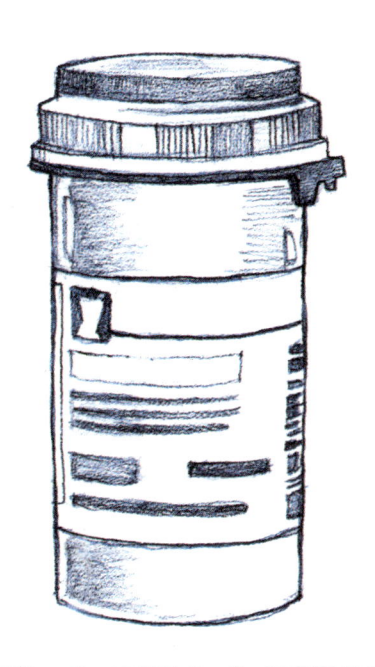

PROTECTED MEDICARE

Health care reform has already saved more than 5.2 million seniors and people with disabilities on Medicare $3.7 billion in prescription drug costs, allowed 33 million Medicare recipients to get free preventive services, and reduced Medicare deductibles and even some premiums.[94]

Before health care reform, Medicare was supposed to run out of money in 2016. By cutting out unnecessary payments to insurance companies and cracking down on waste and fraud, the Affordable Care Act extends the life of the Medicare trust fund by eight years.

Before health care reform, Medicare costs were increasing, forcing seniors to pay more and more out of pocket, but Medicare costs for seniors will decrease in 2012. Premiums for prescription drugs and the cost of Medicare Advantage health plans have already dropped. Medicare Part B deductibles fell by $22 between 2011 and 2012, and the 2012 premium increase of $3.50 for most seniors was much lower than expected. Many actually saw their premiums decrease.[95]

Before health care reform, millions of seniors fell into the Medicare prescription drug coverage gap or "donut hole" every year, forcing them to pay out of pocket, sometimes thousands of dollars. Today these seniors are able to get big discounts, including 50 percent on brand-name prescriptions and up to 14 percent on generic drugs, saving more than $600 a year on average.

Before health care reform, Medicare did not cover an annual checkup, and seniors could pay hundreds of dollars for important preventive screenings. Today, free preventive services include annual wellness visits, flu shots, cholesterol and blood pressure checks, mammograms, bone density screenings, colon cancer screenings, and smoking cessation counseling.

According to the Centers for Medicare & Medicaid Services, health care reform will save Medicare more than $200 billion through 2016 by reducing excessive Medicare payments to the private insurers who participate in Medicare Advantage, reforming provider payments, improving patient safety, and cracking down on fraud and abuse.

Health care reform guarantees that Medicare-covered benefits won't be reduced or taken away, and seniors will always be able to choose their own doctor.

But without health care reform, a retired couple could expect to pay an additional $20,000 in medical bills.[96] And forget about all those benefits listed above.

Hey Mitt: Remember, Seniors Vote!

REASON 18

THE STOCK MARKET

The Stock Market

In the first quarter of 2012, the Dow Jones Industrial Average and the S&P 500 posted their best quarters in nearly fourteen years, while the NASDAQ had its best quarter since 1991. The Dow is currently about double the level it was in March 2009, shortly after Obama became president. Since Obama became president on January 20, 2009, the stock market has risen at an annual rate of 16.4 percent, even after adjusting for inflation. Obama has presided over the fifth best stock market record of any president, behind Franklin D. Roosevelt, Calvin Coolidge, Bill Clinton, and Dwight D. Eisenhower.[97]

The Dow Jones Industrial Average has surged 60 percent since Barack Obama was inaugurated as president more than three years ago. Obama is one of only five presidents to see the stock market increase more than 50 percent during his first three years in office.[98]

What's more, the stock market performs better under Democratic presidents than Republican. Looking back fifty years, we see annualized returns of 11 percent under the past twenty-three years of Democratic presidents since Kennedy, compared to only 2.7 percent under the past twenty-eight years of Republican presidents.[99]

In fact, according to Professor Robert Prechter of the Socionomics Institute, in a March 2012 study entitled, "Social Mood, Stock Market Performance and U.S. Presidential Elections: A Socionomic Perspective on Voting Results," Obama is headed for a landslide reelection. Prechter's research shows that social mood as reflected by the stock market is a more powerful predictor of reelection outcomes than economic variables such as GDP, inflation, or unemployment:

> We define a large positive stock market change as a net gain of 20% or more in the preceding three-year period. . . . We conclude that a large net positive stock market change during the three years prior to the election is highly likely to be associated with a landslide victory for the incumbent.

I'm a Taurus . . . why argue with the bulls?

REASON 19

RESPONSIBLE IMMIGRATION REFORM

[W]e are the first nation to be founded for the sake of an idea—the idea that each of us deserves the chance to shape our own destiny. That is why centuries of pioneers and immigrants have risked everything to come here.

—President Barack Obama, State of the Union Address, January 25, 2011[100]

We are indeed a nation of immigrants. For too long, our country has failed to address the very real need for comprehensive immigration reform. We have allowed politics to get in the way of progress, and millions have suffered as a result. That's why President Obama announced this June that undocumented youths who came here as children would no longer be deported under certain conditions.

To qualify, individuals must be no older than thirty, and younger than sixteen, when they arrived in the United States; have been here at least five years; be enrolled in school, have graduated from high school, or have served in the military; and have no felony or serious misdemeanor convictions. An estimated 700,000 K to 12 students, including 150,000 currently enrolled in high school, could benefit, according to the Pew Hispanic Center. Up to 1.4 million young immigrants in total may qualify.

President Obama took this extraordinary step in the face of a Republican Congress that has refused to do anything on immigration, including passing the DREAM Act, which would give undocumented students who came to the United States as minors the chance to obtain permanent U.S. residency if they go to college or serve in the military, and to eventually apply for citizenship if they desire.

In the absence of a legal path to citizenship, which Republicans have consistently blocked, the temporary measure President Obama has taken will remove the threat of deportation for two years, after which time individuals would need to reapply. Speaking about why he made this decision, he said:

> I've met these young people all across the country. They're studying in our schools. They're playing with our children, pledging allegiance to our flag, hoping to serve our country. They are Americans in their hearts, in their minds. They are Americans through and through— in every single way but on paper. And all they want is to go to college and give back to the country they love.[101]

In addition, to make it easier for undocumented immigrants who are immediate family members of American citizens to apply for permanent residency, President Obama is proposing to allow them to stay in the United States while they apply, a move that could affect as many as one million of the estimated eleven million immigrants living here illegally. Under the current process, those applying for citizenship may be separated from their families for long stretches of time, as many as ten years. This reform would cut down that time to as little as a week apart under a "hardship waiver."

President Obama has also prioritized border security, with twice as many border patrol agents now as in 2004,[102] and today there are fewer illegal crossings than at any time in the past forty years. The administration has focused on deporting criminals who threaten our communities, and such deportations are up 80 percent.

Mitt Romney has promised to veto the DREAM Act, supports "self-deportation," and calls Arizona's recent law, which makes it a crime to be an undocumented immigrant and requires police to check the immigration status of anyone they stop if they suspect the person may be in the country illegally, a "model for the country on immigration."

Even the conservative U.S. Supreme Court struck down most of the provisions of this draconian law that Romney has enthusiastically supported. Obama has condemned this legislation since it was first passed.

Barack Obama is committed to securing our borders and establishing a path to citizenship for those responsible immigrants already in this country. Mitt Romney seems intent on becoming the most anti-immigrant U.S. presidential candidate in modern history.

REASON 20

COMMANDER IN CHIEF FOR THE TWENTY-FIRST CENTURY

COMMANDER IN CHIEF

For the first time in nine years, there are no Americans fighting in Iraq. For the first time in two decades, Osama bin Laden is not a threat to this country. Most of al-Qaida's top lieutenants have been defeated. The Taliban's momentum has been broken, and some troops in Afghanistan have begun to come home.

—President Barack Obama, State of the Union Address, January 24, 2012[103]

Barack Obama has proven himself to be an extraordinary commander in chief. From Iraq and Afghanistan to fighting terrorism and reducing the nuclear threat, President Obama understands how to project and utilize force to strengthen our national security, protect our homeland, reinforce our alliances, and preserve taxpayer dollars.

President Obama's most impressive achievements as commander in chief:

1. Killed Osama bin Laden
2. Ended the Iraq war
3. Established exit plan for Afghanistan
4. Personally approves hits on terrorists and has executed at least 266 drone strikes in Pakistan[104]
5. Rescued kidnapped Americans held hostage by Somali pirates
6. Helped overthrow Muammar Qaddafi
7. Negotiated the first nuclear arms reduction treaty in twenty years
8. Won the Nobel Peace Prize
9. Restored America's leadership on the world stage
10. Regularly visits troops in Iraq and Afghanistan and improves veterans' lives at home

Not bad for a guy with no military background.

Smart strategy + Strong leadership = A more secure world.

REASON 21

KEEPING OUR HOMES

KEEPING OUR HOMES

Six weeks after taking office, President Obama introduced the Making Home Affordable program (MHA) to help homeowners prevent foreclosure, stabilize the housing market, and improve our economy. Under this program, many homeowners can lower their monthly mortgage payments. If they can no longer afford, or no longer desire, homeownership, there is a program that can help them avoid foreclosure and provide a responsible way out. Other options exist for homeowners who owe more than their homes are worth or are unemployed. Through these efforts, Obama has already helped over a million homeowners keep their homes and save billions of dollars, and with the extension of some of these programs through the end of 2013, millions more may be able to do the same—as long as he remains in the White House.

Two months later, in May 2009, Obama signed the Helping Families Save Their Homes Act and the Fraud Enforcement and Recovery Act. The Helping Families Save Their Homes Act made it easier to use the Making Home Affordable program, established protections for renters living in foreclosed homes, and ensured that homeowners can easily find out who owns their mortgage. It also provided $2.2 billion to fight homelessness. The Fraud Enforcement and Recovery Act enables the federal government to crack down on the kind of fraud, manipulation, and predatory lending that put thousands of working families, in spite of doing everything right, at risk of losing their homes.

In February 2012, Obama unveiled a new mortgage refinancing proposal, calling it a "make or break" for the middle class. According to the president, the plan

> will give every responsible homeowner the chance to save about $3,000 a year on their mortgages by refinancing at historically low rates. No more red tape. No more endless forms. And a small fee on the largest financial institutions will make sure it doesn't add a dime to the deficit.[105]

President Obama also proposed a "Homeowner's Bill of Rights" that requires simple mortgages with no hidden fees, guidelines to prevent conflicts of interest damaging to homeowners, support for families who are current on their mortgage payments, and protection against inappropriate foreclosure. Obama also announced a pilot program to convert foreclosed properties into rental homes to improve neighborhoods and home prices.[106]

The Results: As of April 2012, over one million homeowners have received a permanent modification through the Home Affordable Modification Program, the largest MHA program. These homeowners have reduced their monthly mortgage payments by one-third—a median of approximately $535—saving an estimated total of $12.7 billion to date. Those homeowners with the principal reduction alternative feature have reduced the median amount of their principal by $68,267.[107]

The application deadline for the program has been extended to December 31, 2013, and the eligibility criteria have been expanded, making it easier to qualify, especially if you are in the armed forces.

There are also signs that the housing market is finally coming back to life. As the *New York Times* reported in June 2012, home prices are rising, sales are increasing, and home builders are reporting increased activity. "Our sense is that the market is recovering, and we're extremely confident that it's not going to get worse," said Ronnie Morgan, a San Diego real estate agent. "It feels very much like we've hit a bottom and we're starting to come off of that bottom," said Stuart Miller, chief executive of Lennar, a major national home builder based in Miami.[108]

This past June the National Association of Realtors showed the highest level of pending home sales in almost two years. Other signs that point to a stronger housing market, with more buyers, include: rising rents and low mortgage rates; an economy that has continued to improve while home prices have fallen; population growth without significant new construction; and housing stock for sale continuing to decline.[109]

What's more, owners' equity in household real estate has held steady since President Obama took office, after falling more than 50 percent from its peak in 2006, according to the Federal Reserve.[110]

Mitt Romney's Response: "Don't try and stop the foreclosure process. Let it run its course and hit the bottom."[111] He favors allowing investors to make money while families get kicked out on the street.

Message to Mitt: Keep your house, 'cause you ain't movin' to the White House!

REASON 22

$1 TRILLION IN SPENDING CUTS

Over the next ten years, President Obama's proposed budget, which includes $1.1 trillion in spending cuts, is projected to cut the deficit by nearly half, reducing it by $626 billion from $1.33 trillion, to $704 billion. Obama's budget includes more than $4 trillion in balanced deficit reduction, so that by 2018, the deficit will be less than 3 percent of GDP. For every $1 in new revenue generated from the new taxes on those making over $250,000 per year, and from closing corporate loopholes, the budget has $2.50 in spending cuts, including the deficit reduction enacted over the last year.[112]

The $1 trillion in spending cuts includes savings of $350 billion from defense over the next decade—the first defense cut since the 1990s. In addition to deficit reduction, Obama plans to use part of these savings from bringing troops home to pay for much-needed infrastructure improvements, such as modernizing the nation's transportation network, which will create hundreds of thousands of jobs.

The Budget Control Act of 2011 signed by President Obama immediately enacted ten-year discretionary spending caps generating nearly $1 trillion in deficit reduction, which are balanced between defense and nondefense spending.

According to the White House, the president's 2013 budget "would bring discretionary spending to its lowest level as a share of the economy since Dwight D. Eisenhower sat in the Oval Office."[113] Obama specifically identifies 210 places where programs would be cut or eliminated, for savings of $520 billion over a decade.

So far, Barack Obama has signed $2 trillion of spending cuts into law, and spending under the Obama administration has grown more slowly than under any president in sixty years. In fact, federal spending grew about six times faster under Reagan and Bush than it has grown under Obama.[114]

Now that's a record even The Gipper would be proud of!

REASON 23

EQUAL PAY FOR WOMEN

Right now, women are a growing number of breadwinners in the household. But they're still earning just 77 cents for every dollar a man does—even less if you're an African American or Latina woman. Overall, a woman with a college degree doing the same work as a man will earn hundreds of thousands of dollars less over the course of her career. So closing this pay gap—ending pay discrimination— is about far more than simple fairness. When more women are bringing home the bacon, but bringing home less of it than men who are doing the same work, that weakens families, it weakens communities, it's tough on our kids, it weakens our entire economy.

—President Barack Obama, April 6, 2012[115]

Nine days after Barack Obama was sworn into office, he signed his first bill into law, the Lilly Ledbetter Fair Pay Act, as a direct response to a May 2007 Supreme Court ruling that made it harder for employees to file pay discriminations claims.

Ledbetter worked as an overnight supervisor (7 p.m. to 7 a.m.) for nearly two decades at the Alabama Goodyear Tire and Rubber Company, and she suffered sexual harassment and day-to-day discrimination. A supervisor once asked for sexual favors in return for a good evaluation. Not long before Ledbetter was going to retire in 1998, an anonymous coworker put a note in her mailbox at work comparing her pay against that of three male counterparts. Ledbetter was making $3,727 per month, while men doing the same job were paid $4,286 to $5,236 per month. Ledbetter filed a complaint with the Equal Employment Opportunity Commission, and she was then assigned to lift heavy tires. Ledbetter sued Goodyear, which claimed it paid her less than male employees because she was not a good worker, despite having received a top performance award in 1996. The Supreme Court voted 5–4 that Ledbetter was not entitled to compensation because she filed her claim more than 180 days after receiving her first discriminatory paycheck. She lost more than $200,000 in wages and benefits during her career due to gender discrimination.

The Lilly Ledbetter Fair Pay Act amends the 1964 Civil Rights Act to allow for claims within 180 days of each check considered discriminatory. To further enhance enforcement of equal pay laws nationwide, President Obama established the Equal Pay Task Force in 2010.

In April this year, Diane Sawyer asked Mitt Romney, "If you were president—you had been president—would you have signed the Lilly Ledbetter Law?"

He refused to answer the question.[116]

Who do you trust more to protect the rights of women?

REASON 24

SUPREME COURT APPOINTMENTS

In perhaps no greater sphere do presidents have a longer-lasting impact than in the judiciary, particularly the Supreme Court. Decisions made by an appointee to the Supreme Court can have consequences decades after a president leaves office. Rulings by the Court affect every aspect of American society and can touch literally every man, woman, and child in the country.

Ruth Bader Ginsburg plans to retire in 2015, giving Obama his third appointee if reelected. Electing Romney would be devastating to the future of the Supreme Court and the country. If Romney is elected and Ginsburg retires, over the next four years a real shift in power would occur. Romney is likely to appoint an ultraconservative who will cement right-wing domination of the Court, likely leading to decisions against choice, affirmative action, and the freedom to marry, among other issues.

In contrast, look no further than Sonia Sotomayor, Obama's first Supreme Court appointment, the first nominee by a Democratic president in fifteen years. Sotomayor, like Obama, is the embodiment of the America Dream. The first Latina on the Court, she was raised by a single mother in a Bronx housing project and worked her way up to graduate from Princeton University and Yale Law School.

Obama's second Supreme Court appointment was Elena Kagan, who represents a newer, younger perspective, drawing more from experiences outside the courtroom as well as knowledge of the law. Kagan and Sotomayor, along with Ginsburg and Stephen Breyer, provide a liberal counterweight to the extreme conservative bloc that includes Clarence Thomas, Antonin Scalia, John Roberts, and Samuel Alito. Anthony Kennedy is considered the lone "swing" vote.

According to an analysis by the *New York Times*, four of the six most conservative justices who have sat on the court since 1937 are serving now (Roberts, Alito, Scalia, Thomas). Even

Justice Kennedy is in the top ten.[117] Any more conservative appointments would tip the Court so far to the right it might fall over.

One need only examine the recent ruling upholding the centerpiece of the unfair and draconian Arizona immigration law, which requires police to check the immigration status of anyone they stop or arrest if they have a reasonable suspicion that the person may be an illegal immigrant. And while a bare majority upheld the health care law, the Court may have dramatically limited the scope of the Commerce Clause, a provision Congress has used since the 1820s to expand protections for citizens. Justice Ginsburg warned that the Court's Commerce Clause ruling was "a stunning step back that should not have staying power."[118]

An Obama victory this November is absolutely essential to protect the rights of *all* Americans, for decades and decades to come.

REASON 25

SUPPORTS SCIENCE THAT'S HELPING EVERY AMERICAN

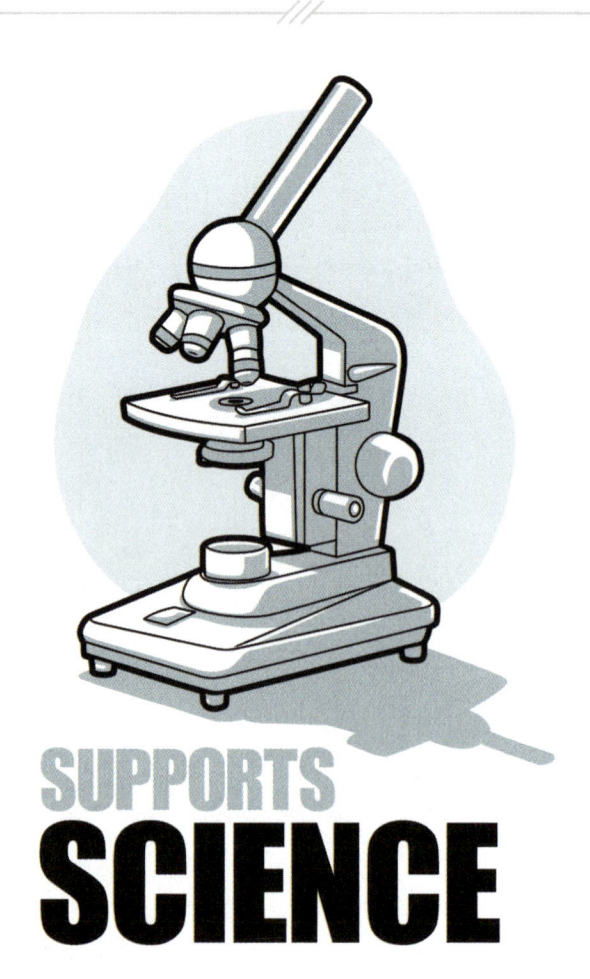

SUPPORTS SCIENCE

I'm a Christian, and I believe in parents being able to provide children with religious instruction without interference from the state. But I also believe our schools are there to teach worldly knowledge and science. I believe in evolution, and I believe there's a difference between science and faith. That doesn't make faith any less important than science. It just means they're two different things. And I think it's a mistake to try to cloud the teaching of science with theories that frankly don't hold up to scientific inquiry.

—President Barack Obama[119]

Amazing that in 2012 we are still having this debate, but Yes, Virginia, Science is real.[120]

Fortunately, Obama can differentiate between science and religion, and understands the need to strengthen *"America's role as the world's engine of scientific discovery and technological innovation."*[121]

On the other hand, Mitt Romney and many Republicans have compromised their principles and their beliefs in a hypocritical and crass attempt to pander and placate the increasingly intolerant religious right.

This antiscience attack has serious implications, particularly on issues such as education, global warming, and medical research.

Education

Early in his administration, Obama launched the Educate to Innovate campaign to help move U.S. students from mediocre ratings internationally in science and math achievement to the head of the class during the next decade. The effort includes

$260 million in partnerships involving the federal government, companies, foundations, nonprofits, universities, and science and engineering societies to prepare more than 10,000 new math and science teachers and train more than 100,000 current teachers.[122]

Global Warming

Mitt Romney has loudly proclaimed his doubts about global warming science, saying, *"My view is that we don't know what's causing climate change on this planet."*[123] Of course, that was only a few months after he said, "I believe the world is getting warmer. . . . I believe that humans contribute to that."[124] So, in fact, we really don't know *what* Mitt Romney truly believes about the causes of global warming.

In contrast, Barack Obama has always been very clear on his position, unequivocally stating when first running for president that "global warming is real, is happening now, and is the result of human activities."[125] As president, Obama has actively fought against global warming by:

- Reengaging in the agreements and talks on global warming and greenhouse gas emissions.
- Pledging a 28 percent cut in federal greenhouse gas emissions by 2020.
- Regulating greenhouse gases for large industrial sources.
- Establishing the first-ever greenhouse gas emission levels for passenger cars and light trucks.

Medical Research

Less than two months into his term, President Obama overturned Bush's ban limiting stem cell research. According to the UK newspaper *The Telegraph*, this decision helped lead to the first study "showing that cells derived from human embryonic stem cells can be transplanted safely into a patient, with no sign of complications." In this case, two legally blind women "saw their vision improve in a matter of weeks after being given the embryo-derived cells in a U.S. safety trial."[126]

President Obama included $5 billion in grants to fund innovative medical research in all fifty states as part of the Recovery Act. The more than twelve thousand grants will create tens of thousands of jobs, and it includes more than $1 billion to identify new gene-based treatments for cancer, heart disease, and autism.[127]

The Republican war on science has significant consequences for our children, our environment, and our health. The triumph of science will create jobs, enhance our lives, and better our world. The death of science will imperil our nation, limit our future, and cast us alongside backward theocracies like Iran.

Which side are you on?

REASON 26

REPEAL OF "DON'T ASK, DON'T TELL"

DON'T ASK, DON'T TELL

No longer will our nation be denied the service of thousands of patriotic Americans forced to leave the military, despite years of exemplary performance, because they happen to be gay. And no longer will many thousands more be asked to live a lie in order to serve the country they love.

—President Barack Obama, December 18, 2010[128]

In February 2008, then-Senator Barack Obama released an open letter to the LGBT community in which he called for the repeal of Don't Ask, Don't Tell, the policy that prohibited openly gay, lesbian, or bisexual persons from military service. He reiterated that promise during the 2010 State of the Union address, saying he would "work with Congress and our military to finally repeal the law that denies gay Americans the right to serve the country they love because of who they are."

Our country is safer, our military force is stronger, and our national character is strengthened as a result of the end of DADT.

Our government will no longer waste hundreds of millions of taxpayer dollars enforcing an unnecessary, ineffective, and unpopular policy that undermined our military readiness and our national security by asking gay service members to live a lie. The repeal of DADT will enhance military readiness and strengthen national security while upholding America's ideals, namely the belief that all men and women are created equal. For decades, gay men and women have risked their lives in silence to serve our country, and now they can do so openly, honestly, and with the dignity, integrity, and respect the uniform deserves.

The costs of DADT:

- Between 1993 and 2011, 14,356 qualified service members were discharged because of their sexuality—the equivalent of an entire division of fighters.[129]
- Of those men and women discharged, 2,215 filled critical roles in the service branches, including voice interceptors, data-processing technicians, translators, and special security forces.[130]
- More than $600 million was spent to discharge and replace these service members, at a cost of $52,800 each.[131]
- Annually, 4,000 gay men and women refused to reenlist due to the DADT policy.[132]

For years, conservative opponents warned that open service would lead to a mass exodus of troops opposed to repeal of DADT, and that it would also push away potential recruits opposed to open service. There have never been any reputable or peer-reviewed studies that have shown that allowing service by openly gay personnel compromises military cohesion or effectiveness.

Indeed, the facts plainly tell the story. Reports from the Pentagon clearly demonstrate that each branch of the military exceeded its recruitment goals for fiscal year 2011—most of which took place after repeal became law. All branches also met their fiscal 2011 retention goals, except for the air force, which retained 96 percent of its members.[133]

The Defense Department's numbers, as well as opinion polls of troops conducted by the military and outside sources, prove that allowing gay men and women to serve openly never posed a threat to recruitment or retention.[134] Open service actually improves our military's ability to recruit troops by expanding the pool of potential candidates to include the many thousands of gay Americans willing to serve their country. It also improves our military's readiness by not forcing otherwise qualified troops out of service simply because of who they are.

America was at war for nearly half the time DADT was in effect. The policy actually threatened unit cohesion by requiring certain service members to intentionally mislead their fellow troops and officers, undermining core military values of honesty and integrity and potentially distracting troops from successfully completing the mission at hand. Moreover, thousands of personnel with mission-critical skills, including Arab linguists and combat engineers, were abruptly and unfairly forced out of the military, just when their service was needed most.

With the repeal of DADT, military policy is now properly aligned with military values. And America's policy is consistent with that of many of our closest allies, including the United Kingdom, France, Germany, and Israel.

As if we need any further proof that ending DADT was the right thing to do, here are some of the countries that still ban gays from serving in the military: Cuba, China, Egypt, Iran, North Korea, Saudi Arabia, Somalia, Sudan, Syria, Uganda, Venezuela, and Yemen. Nice group to be associated with . . . *not!*

REASON 27

MITT ROMNEY

There are so many reasons not to vote for Mitt Romney. Here are my top seven:

1. His Economic Plan

Mitt Romney believes the best way to grow the economy is from the top down. Cut taxes for the wealthy and eliminate regulations on banks, polluters, and insurance and oil companies. Romney wants to keep all of the Bush tax cuts, and then add another $5 trillion on top of that, with 70 percent of those tax cuts going to people making $200,000 or more a year, according to the White House. Folks making over a million dollars a year would get a 25 percent tax cut, on average. To pay for this, the White House says, Romney would need to cut nearly a trillion dollars from the part of the budget that includes everything from education and job training to medical research and clean energy, the deepest cuts in modern times.

If that cut was spread evenly across the budget, White House calculations show, ten million college students would lose about $1,000 each in financial aid and two hundred thousand children would get kicked out of Head Start programs. There would be sixteen hundred fewer medical research grants for things like Alzheimer's, cancer, and AIDS, and forty-eight thousand researchers would lose their grants. Over fifty million Americans would lose their health insurance, including millions of nursing home patients, as well as families who have children with autism and other disabilities.

According to the nonpartisan Tax Policy Center, Mitt Romney would give those in the top 20 percent an average tax cut of more than $16,000 while raising taxes on the bottom 20 percent of workers. The top 1 percent would get a cut of almost $150,000 per year, and the top 0.1 percent would receive a whopping $725,000 reduction, on average. The Tax Policy Center confirmed that Romney's plan would add at least $4 trillion to the deficit.[135]

Moody's said the following about Mr. Romney's plan: "On net, all of these policies would do more harm in the short term.

If we implemented all of his policies, it would push us deeper into recession and make the recovery slower."[136]

Cut taxes for the rich and create a deficit that our grandchildren will have to pay for? No thanks, I think we tried that one before.

2. His Record at Bain Capital

Romney spent fifteen years at Bain Capital, where he succeeded at piling debt on companies, outsourcing jobs to China and India,[137] firing American workers, and leaving many companies in bankruptcy. There's nothing wrong with private equity, whose goal is to maximize profit above all else, but it is hardly a training ground for job creation.

Trying to take credit for jobs created by entrepreneurs he advised or through deals he was tangentially involved in doesn't "pass the laugh test," says *Washington Post* fact-checker Glenn Kessler, who awards Romney three Pinocchios for his job creation claims.[138] As governor of Massachusetts, he ranked forty-seventh out of fifty in job creation.[139]

Even putting aside his record at Bain Capital, Romney places way too much stock in his business experience as preparation for the White House. Bill Clinton, who created the most jobs of any president, had no prior business experience. Ronald Reagan, an actor, presided over a very powerful economic expansion. The two presidents with the most business experience? Herbert Hoover and George W. Bush . . . hardly models for economic prosperity.

3. He's a Flip-Flopper

Where does this guy stand on the issues? He was for a woman's right to choose, now he wants to overturn *Roe v. Wade* and block the government from funding Planned Parenthood. He supported equality for gays and lesbians and now wants to write discrimination into the Constitution and allow states to ban gays from adopting children or visiting their partners in the hospital. He's even against civil unions. He was against all forms of no-tax pledges and now can't wait to sign them. He used to think humans caused global warming, but now he's not so sure. He used to be for gun control, now he's against it.[140] How can you vote for someone when you don't even know what he really believes?

4. He Can't Relate to the 99 Percent

Poll after poll shows that when it comes to likability, Obama wins in a landslide. Likability, or favorability, another common political metric on which Romney trails miserably, is a gut-check measure of how people relate to an individual. Likability and favorability are critically important qualities that presidents use to attract voters, marshal support, and lead the nation. These qualities lead to trust and confidence, which help generate optimism in a nation and create a sense of strength. In a divided government—and a divided nation facing tough choices—the ability to persuade and bring people over to your side is an extraordinary asset to effective governance. Just look at the three past presidents who have been reelected—Reagan, Clinton, George W. Bush—all extremely likable. Romney's favorability ratings have consistently been under water, with more Americans viewing him unfavorably than favorably.[141] No candidate in the modern polling era with personal favorability ratings as low as his has ever won the presidency. Romney is on track to be the most unpopular presidential nominee on record.

Then there's the enthusiasm gap. People just aren't psyched about supporting Romney: 93 percent of those who support Obama are excited about supporting him, while only 75 percent of Romney supporters are enthusiastic about their candidate.[142] To put that in perspective, in June 2008, Obama's enthusiasm rating was 91 percent and McCain's was 74 percent . . . and we all know how that election turned out.

People voting for Romney don't even like him, they just dislike Obama. Of those who would vote for Romney in an April 2012 poll, 63 percent were voting against Obama and only 35 percent were voting for Romney. Among Obama voters, 76 percent were voting for Obama, while only 23 percent were voting against Romney.[143]

5. He's Committed to Inequality

- "Not concerned about the very poor"[144]
- Thinks the middle class is "envious" of the 1 percent
- Believes that income inequality should be discussed in "quiet rooms"[145]
- Silent on equal pay for women
- Opposes the freedom to marry and civil unions for gay and lesbian couples
- Opposes a path to citizenship for undocumented immigrants, even those who came here as children and now want to go to college or serve in the military[146]

6. He's Become Ultraconservative to Appeal to the Far Right

Compared to George W. Bush, Mitt Romney is an ultraconservative.[147]

- Bush passed a huge tax cut that America couldn't afford, mostly benefiting the wealthy. According to the Center for American Progress, Romney's tax cut plan is four times larger ($10.7 trillion in tax cuts over ten years), and almost three times more beneficial to the superrich (33 percent benefiting the top one tenth of 1 percent).[148] Millionaires would save over $250,535, on average.[149]
- Bush signed the McCain-Feingold campaign finance law. Romney wants to repeal virtually all campaign finance laws.[150]
- Bush supported comprehensive immigration reform, a path to citizenship for twelve million undocumented immigrants, and portions of the DREAM Act (Development, Relief, and Education for Alien Minors). Romney opposes all of these measures.
- Bush expanded Medicare by providing seniors with prescription drug benefits. Romney wants to end Medicare as we know it.
- Bush raised the minimum wage. Romney opposes increasing the minimum wage.

- Bush enacted higher fuel efficiency standards. Romney says even current standards are too high.
- Bush admitted global warming is caused by humans. Romney says, "We don't know what's causing climate change."[151]
- Bush approved one of the biggest land conservation programs in U.S. history. Romney thinks the federal government owns too much land.
- Bush supported civil unions for gay and lesbian couples. Romney opposes them.

Mitt Romney: The most conservative Republican nominee since Barry Goldwater.

7. He Would Be a Foreign Policy and National Security Nightmare

- Thinks Russia is "our number one geopolitical foe,"[152] worse than Iran, North Korea, or China
- Advisors are the same ultra-right-wing neocons who got us into the Iraq war
- Engages in reckless warmongering talk on Iran
- Opposed to a political settlement in Afghanistan
- Doesn't understand that China's threat is primarily economic, not military
- Wants to take a backseat in the Middle East
- Wants to increase military spending by $2.1 trillion over the next decade . . .

Wait, aren't we supposed to be cutting spending?

REASON 28

KEPT HIS CAMPAIGN PROMISES

Over the course of a campaign, presidential candidates make hundreds of promises, so many in fact that it's hard to keep count.

Good thing we have PolitiFact, an independent, Pulitzer Prize–winning project of the *Tampa Bay Times*. PolitiFact "help(s) you find the truth in [American] politics. Every day reporters and help(s) you find the truth in [American] politics. Every day, reporters and researchers from PolitiFact and its partner news organizations examine statements by members of Congress, state legislators, governors, mayors, the president, cabinet secretaries, lobbyists . . . We research their statements and then rate the accuracy on our Truth-O-Meter."[153]

They have also been tracking more than *five hundred* promises that Barack Obama made on the campaign trail, and the results may surprise even the most fervent Obama supporter.

As president, Barack Obama has kept, compromised, or is currently working on an astounding *74 percent* of his campaign promises, the equivalent of a Presidential batting title. Another 12 percent are stalled, often in the face of Congressional inaction.[154]

Just looking at the pledges that PolitiFact judged as the most important of the campaign, the president has an equally compelling record, delivering in some way on twenty of the top twenty-five.

What's all the more impressive is that the president was able to amass such an impressive record in the face of extraordinary resistance from a Republican House that frequently voted against him on party-line votes, and a Senate where sixty votes are often necessary to get anything done.

Barack Obama keeps his promises.

Mitt Romney seems to have trouble even remembering the promises he's made.

So who ya gonna trust?

REASON 29

FORWARD VERSUS BACKWARD

There is no question that this election presents us with one of the starkest choices we have faced in generations. At its core, America must decide whether it wants to move Forward or Backward.

On issues ranging from equality and civil rights to economics and foreign policy, Mitt Romney has made it clear that he wants to take America backward.

Romney is opposed not only to same-sex marriage, which President Obama supports, but also to civil unions for gays and lesbians, something which even George W. Bush supported. In fact, Romney supports a constitutional amendment stating that marriage should only be between a man and woman, an issue that Congress has ignored since it failed by over fifty votes more than six years ago. Romney even thinks that issues like hospital visitation rights should be left to the states to decide, despite the fact that more than eight in ten Americans support visitation rights for gays and lesbians.

Romney has failed to say whether or not he would have signed the Lilly Ledbetter Fair Pay Act. This act amends the Civil Rights Act of 1964 by clarifying that the 180-day statute of limitations for filing an equal-pay lawsuit regarding pay discrimination resets with each new discriminatory paycheck.

On military and foreign policy, Romney wants to take us back to the days of Bush, complete with unilateralism, massive military budgets, and bellicose warmongering talk. The journalist James Traub has dubbed Romney's approach to foreign affairs, the "more enemies, fewer friends" doctrine.[155] In *The American Conservative*, Daniel Larison recently wrote of Romney:

> He will wreck the relationship with Russia, he won't negotiate with the Taliban, and he will be more likely to order an attack on Iran (and he believes he can do this

on his own authority). The trouble is that Romney makes statements that seem so far removed from reality that journalists and pundits usually just shrug their shoulders and dismiss it as campaign hyperbole. They say to themselves, "No one could be foolish enough to do what he says he'll do!" Romney has been able to brush off a series of foreign policy blunders that would normally be considered major liabilities if they had been made by someone who was supposed to know what he was talking about. Romney's inexperience and incompetence on foreign policy have become very effective political shields.[156]

Perhaps most troubling, Romney has made it clear that he will take us back to Bush's economic policies, which almost exclusively benefited the wealthy upper class. This April, Alexandra Franceschi, a spokesperson for the Republican National Committee, said that the Republican Party's economic platform in 2012 was going to be the same as it was during the Bush years, "just updated."[157] This admission is particularly frightening, given that Bush produced the lowest increase in investment, GDP, and employment of any postwar expansion, with monthly job growth the worst since at least February 1945, household income dropping for the first time since tracking began, and the deficit and debt exploding. It would have to be quite the update for the GOP to make anything better happen this time around. No wonder why Bill Clinton has called these "the same ideas they've tried before, except on steroids."

In a June 2012 speech, President Obama succinctly assessed the damage caused during the Bush era:

> We were told that huge tax cuts—especially for the wealthiest Americans—would lead to faster job growth. We were told that fewer regulations—especially for big financial institutions and corporations—would bring about widespread prosperity. We were told that it was OK to put two wars on the nation's credit card; that tax cuts would create enough growth to pay for themselves. So

how did this economic theory work out? For the wealthiest Americans it worked out pretty well. . . . But prosperity never trickled down to the middle class.[158]

As Treasury Secretary Timothy Geithner said, the Republican approach "is a recipe to make us a declining power, a less exceptional nation, and it's a dark and pessimistic vision of America."[159]

Romney wants to take us back to the days of Bush: tax cuts for the wealthy, equality for some, health care for the few, economic growth for no one, and risky foreign policy for us all.

President Obama wants to move us forward: a stronger middle class, quality health care that's affordable, a twenty-first-century educational system, expanded opportunities for every American, and a safer world for us all.

REASON 30

A TRUE LEADER

We lose ourselves when we compromise the very ideals that we fight to defend. And we honor those ideals by upholding them not when it's easy, but when it is hard.

—Barack Obama, accepting the
Nobel Peace Prize, December 10, 2009[160]

What is the mark of a true leader?

- makes hard decisions even when they are unpopular
- stands by principles and follows through
- takes risks

In five key areas, Barack Obama has shown himself to be an extraordinary leader:

1. Sending Thirty Thousand Additional Troops to Afghanistan

Despite strong opposition from his own party, Vice President Biden, and his chief of staff, President Obama ordered thirty thousand more troops to be sent to Afghanistan in December 2009, raising the total number of troops there to more than one hundred thousand, an increase of more than sixty thousand since he took office earlier that year. He accelerated the timetable of the deployment, sending the troops there more quickly than initially anticipated. But the president also set a clear timetable for the beginning of troop withdrawals, a commitment he kept by starting to bring them home from Afghanistan in July 2011. In May 2012, he signed a strategic partnership agreement with Afghan president Hamid Karzai, ensuring that all combat troops would be withdrawn by 2014 and establishing a solid foundation to guide our commitment to Afghanistan for the next decade.

2. Saving GM and Chrysler

Though most Americans and nearly all Republicans were against the auto bailout, President Obama recognized that letting Detroit go bankrupt, as Mitt Romney had suggested, would destroy the American automotive industry and wreak tremendous havoc on the entire U.S. economy. Over a million jobs would have been lost, and the federal government would have been stuck with paying a $14.5 billion tab for the two companies' pension plans. Today GM is back as the world's number one auto manufacturer and more profitable than ever,[161] and the auto industry has created 230,000 jobs in three years (the most in a decade). All loans have been repaid to the government.

3. Pushing Health Care Reform

During the 2008 campaign, Barack Obama repeatedly pledged to sign a universal health care bill into law by the end of his first term as president. In the face of staunch opposition from Republicans, President Obama realized that if he wanted to deliver on his promise, he would have to push through health care reform immediately, while he had Democratic majorities in both houses of Congress, or risk losing the opportunity, as had so many presidents before him. Fighting against near unanimous opposition from Republicans, unprecedented lobbying by the insurance industry, and pushback from the more liberal wing of his own party, Obama signed the Affordable Care Act just a little over a year after taking office. In summer 2012, the Supreme Court upheld the law.

4. Osama bin Laden Raid

Many of his top advisors, including Vice President Biden, Defense Secretary Robert Gates, and Vice Chairman of the Joint Chiefs of Staff James Cartwright, were against the attack. Bush's secretary of defense, Donald Rumsfeld, had called off a similar raid six years earlier. Success was far from guaranteed, and the costs of failure would have been enormous. But President Obama was convinced that the raid was the only option to ensure that the United States could finally remove the threat posed by Osama bin Laden, and he alone made the call to send in SEAL Team Six.

5. The Stimulus Plan

Facing the greatest economic crisis in eighty years, Barack Obama signed the American Recovery and Reinvestment Act less than a month after being sworn into office. The package of tax cuts, aid to the states, and investment in infrastructure cut taxes for 95 percent of working Americans, saved as many as 3.5 million jobs (according to the nonpartisan Congressional Budget Office), and is credited with preventing another Great Depression. The bill passed the House without a single Republican vote. Since then, the U.S. economy has experienced eleven consecutive quarters of expansion and registered twenty-eight straight months of private-sector job growth, adding 4.4 million new jobs.

Character. Strength. Determination. Perseverance. . . . These are the qualities of a true leader.

REASON 31

FUEL STANDARDS DOUBLING

FUEL STANDARDS DOUBLING

In April 2011, President Obama announced a historic deal with automakers. The agreement calls for an increase in fuel efficiency and reduced greenhouse gas pollution for all new cars and trucks sold in the United States, and the accord represents the most ambitious effort yet to increase fuel economy in America. These standards cover cars and light trucks for model years 2012 through 2026. By 2025, vehicles will be required to achieve 54.5 miles per gallon (more than double our current 27 mpg standard), reducing our dependence on foreign oil, lowering greenhouse gas emissions, and saving Americans billions of dollars in fuel costs.

By 2025, these new standards will reduce oil consumption by an estimated 2.2 million barrels a day—more than we import from any country other than Canada. As older vehicles are replaced with more fuel efficient ones, the oil savings from these standards will grow, ultimately reaching more than four million barrels a day—nearly as much as we import from all OPEC countries combined.

During the life of the program, the standards will cut America's consumption of oil by twelve billion barrels, and cut six billion metric tons of carbon dioxide pollution, equivalent to all the emissions from the United States last year, or what the Amazon rainforest absorbs in three years.

In just a little over a decade, a family that purchases a new vehicle will save $8,200 in fuel costs, compared with a similar vehicle in 2010.[162]

The Natural Resources Defense Council, a leading environmental group, predicts drivers will save an aggregate of $69 billion a year in fuel costs by 2030 because of new gas-mileage standards in cars, or $1.7 trillion at the pump during the life of the program.[163]

At a time when consensus is so hard to achieve in Washington, last year's deal represents an extraordinary compromise among auto manufacturers, environmentalists, and consumer advocates—groups that previously had found little common ground.

President Obama's leadership in rescuing the auto industry, saving American jobs, and preserving American ingenuity paved the way for this historic agreement that benefits consumers, protects the environment, and enhances our security.

Now that's a victory worth celebrating!

REASON 32

LEADERSHIP IN AFGHANISTAN

Today, I signed an historic agreement between the United States and Afghanistan that defines a new kind of relationship between our countries—a future in which Afghans are responsible for the security of their nation, and we build an equal partnership between two sovereign states; a future in which the war ends, and a new chapter begins.

—*President Barack Obama,
Kabul, Afghanistan, May 1, 2012*[164]

In late 2009, President Barack Obama, after careful consideration, ordered another thirty thousand troops be sent to Afghanistan, bringing the total number serving there to over one hundred thousand. The goal was to deny al-Qaeda a safe haven, reverse the Taliban's momentum and prevent it from overthrowing the Afghan government, and strengthen Afghanistan's security forces and government. The move, fiercely debated in Washington, was opposed by many Democrats—including Vice President Biden—and a significant portion of the American people.

At the same time, he set a schedule for withdrawal beginning in mid-2011, a promise that he kept when the first troops began leaving in July 2011. A total of ten thousand left by the end of 2011, and an additional thirty-three thousand troops are scheduled to leave in 2012.

On May 1, 2012, President Obama signed an historic strategic partnership agreement with Afghanistan President Hamid Karzai. The legally binding agreement is

> a signal of the United States' long-term commitment to Afghanistan and represents a common vision for the relationship and Afghanistan's future. . . . The agreement includes mutual commitments in the areas of protecting and promoting shared democratic values, advancing

long-term security, reinforcing regional security and cooperation, supporting social and economic development, and strengthening Afghan institutions and governance.[165]

President Obama made clear that while the United States was not going to abandon Afghanistan when troops are withdrawn in 2014, Afghanistan must take over responsibility for its own security.

With this agreement, the president ensured the continuation and evolution of the American-Afghan relationship even after troops end their combat roles in 2014, and laid the framework for an effective and mutually beneficial long-term relationship between the two countries.

REASON 33

EMBODIMENT OF THE AMERICAN DREAM

Barack Obama is unquestionably the embodiment of the American Dream. He was a middle-class kid raised by a single mom from Kansas, with the help of a grandfather who fought in Patton's army and a Native American grandmother who served on a World War II bomber assembly line, and then worked her way up from the secretarial pool to vice president at a bank.[166]

Obama's mother and father divorced when he was only three years old, and his only memory of his Kenyan father is a one-month visit when Barack was just ten years old. After our future president lived for four years in Indonesia, Barack's mother sent him back to Hawaii to live with his grandparents and attend school. He was reunited with his mom and younger sister a year later when they returned to Hawaii, but when his mom and sister went back to Indonesia three years later, Barack chose to stay with his grandparents and finish high school in America.

Like so many, Obama had to work his way through college with the help of scholarships and student loans. He spent two years at Occidental College in Los Angeles before transferring to Columbia University. After college, he moved to Chicago to work as a community organizer for three years before attending Harvard Law School, where he became the first African American president of the *Harvard Law Review*. From there, he moved back to Chicago to teach, lead a voter registration campaign, and run successfully for the Illinois Senate, U.S. Senate, and eventually, president of the United States. Barack Obama worked his way to the White House not through privilege or paternity, but like many successful leaders, by relying on his own unique mix of guts and grit.

Not bad for a skinny, middle-class, mixed-race, Hawaiian-born kid with a funny name who moved around a lot, huh? Just goes to show what hard work, a strong family, and faith in others can do when you decide to take charge!

REASON 34

CELEBRATION AND ADVANCEMENT OF DIVERSITY

> *Our Nation derives strength from the diversity of its population and from its commitment to equal opportunity for all. We are at our best when we draw on the talents of all parts of our society, and our greatest accomplishments are achieved when diverse perspectives are brought to bear to overcome our greatest challenges.*
>
> —Executive Order 13583—Establishing a Coordinated Government-Wide Initiative to Promote Diversity and Inclusion in the Federal Workforce, August 18, 2011[167]

Barack Obama is the personification of diversity. Son of a white mother from Kansas and a black father from Kenya, his sister is half Indonesian.

From the president's days as a student at Harvard Law, he has prized the power of inclusion, and he protested for more diversity among the Harvard law faculty.[168]

From the start of his presidency, Obama was determined that his administration should look like America. Out of his twenty-two original cabinet members, only nine were white men.

In 2009, the *National Journal* surveyed 366 of Obama's decision makers, people appointed or nominated to senior positions throughout the executive branch. Excluding forty-nine holdovers from the Bush administration, the *Journal* discovered that just under half—49 percent—of the Obama team was white.[169]

Barely four months into his presidency, Obama had the opportunity to nominate a Supreme Court justice, and he picked Sonia Sotomayor. She is not only the first Latina Supreme Court justice and third female justice of the nation's highest court, she is also an embodiment of the American dream, much like Obama.

Sotomayor grew up in the housing projects of the Bronx. Her parents had moved from Puerto Rico during World War II, and they met and married in New York. Her mother served in the Women's Auxiliary Corps. Her father was a tool and die worker with a third-grade education who died when Sotomayor was nine.

According to the *New York Times*, of President Obama's confirmed judiciary nominations, nearly half are women (compared to only 23 percent under Bush); 21 percent are black (7 percent under Bush); and 11 percent are Hispanic (9 percent under Bush).

Obama made history again when J. Paul Oetken became the first openly gay man to be confirmed to the federal judiciary. President Obama has presented three other openly gay nominees to the Senate for consideration. "The president wants the federal courts to look like America," said Kathryn Ruemmler, the White House counsel. "He wants people who are coming to court to feel like it's their court as well."[170]

In response to a 2009 Equal Employment Opportunity Commission annual report on the federal workforce that showed that white men held more than 61 percent of the top or senior-level positions, compared to 29 percent for women, 7 percent for African Americans, and 3.6 percent for Latinos, President Obama issued an executive order requiring federal government agencies to develop and institute plans for increasing diversity within the federal labor pool.[171] The president created the Office of Diversity and Inclusion to boost minority participation in the federal government and to "eliminate demographic group imbalances in targeted occupations and improve workforce diversity."[172] Special initiatives have been created targeting specific groups, including Hispanics, African Americans, Asian Americans, American Indians, Women, the LGBT community, people with disabilities, and veterans.

President Obama understands that the strength of our nation comes from the diversity of our people.

REASON 35

NOBEL PEACE PRIZE

Obama has as President created a new climate in international politics. Multilateral diplomacy has regained a central position, with emphasis on the role that the United Nations and other international institutions can play. Dialogue and negotiations are preferred as instruments for resolving even the most difficult international conflicts. The vision of a world free from nuclear arms has powerfully stimulated disarmament and arms control negotiations. Thanks to Obama's initiative, the USA is now playing a more constructive role in meeting the great climatic challenges the world is confronting.

—The Norwegian Nobel Committee, announcing Obama's 2009 Nobel Peace Prize[173]

Barack Obama received the Nobel Peace Prize less than nine months into his presidency. The committee cited his "extraordinary efforts to strengthen international diplomacy and cooperation between peoples,

The Nobel Committee recognized that Obama had captured the world's imagination and clearly welcomed his multilateral approach and focus on diplomacy and engagement, a radical departure from the Bush administration's bellicose unilateralism, which alienated many in the international community.

Only two other U.S. presidents have received the award while in office: Theodore Roosevelt in 1906 and Woodrow Wilson in 1919.

Obama donated the $1.4 million award to ten charities. The largest portion went to the Fisher House, which provides housing for families of patients receiving medical care at major military and Department of Veteran Affairs medical centers. Another $200,000 went to the Clinton Bush Haiti Fund. Six charities working to prepare students for higher education and help them pay for college each received $125,000: the American Indian College Fund; the Appalachian Leadership and Education Foundation; College Summit; the Hispanic Scholarship Fund; the Posse Foundation; and the United Negro College Fund. Two charities involved in global development each received $100,000: Africare and the Central Asia Institute.[174]

A Nobel Peace Prize winner in the White House . . . Now that's something all Americans can be proud of!

REASON 36

JOE BIDEN

*This is a big f@#%*ng deal*

—Joe Biden, caught on an open mic congratulating President Barack Obama during the health care signing ceremony, Washington, D.C., March 23, 2010[175]

We all know how the vice president is famous for his gaffes. What we may not realize is that Biden has revolutionized the office of the vice presidency, giving it more weight than any other administration in history. He has been more closely involved with a range of day-to-day issues than any of his predecessors and has spearheaded some of the administration's greatest challenges and achievements.

Here are just a few:

- Oversaw implementation of the stimulus plan, creating or saving millions of jobs and helping to rebuild our economy
- Heads the Middle Class Task Force, focusing on education and training, work/family balance, raising middle-class income, restoring labor standards, and protecting retirement security
- Negotiated compromises with Congress on the 2010 tax and 2011 budget packages
- Helped secure the Senate's approval of the New START nuclear-arms reduction treaty with Russia
- Helped end the war in Iraq responsibly, traveling to the country eight times since being elected
- Convinced the president to withdraw troops from Afghanistan

Biden has emerged as Obama's chief troubleshooter and one of his closest advisors. A minister without portfolio, Biden has full access to the president's schedule and can attend any meeting. He is regularly dispatched to deal with some of the administration's thorniest issues, whether they be in China, Pakistan, or on Capitol Hill. Obama and Biden often spend several hours a day together when both are in Washington, and have a weekly one-on-one lunch. Officials say Biden is typically the last person in the room with the president.

"He has a rare ability to understand the political factors which influence the behavior of public officials, both domestic and foreign," says Joel Goldstein, an expert on the vice presidency. "His interpersonal skills have made him well-liked by partisans with whom he has dealt on both sides of the aisle."[176]

Biden sometimes presses Obama to make the tough decision that he knows is right, even if it may not be the best political move. His notorious candor and penchant for off-the-cuff remarks certainly were at play when he helped push Obama out of the closet to publicly declare his support for the freedom to marry.

Joe Biden: strong leader, close advisor, trusted confidant, thoughtful challenger . . . exactly what you want in a vice president.

REASON 37

HILLARY CLINTON

HILLARY CLINTON

Barack Obama's choice of Hillary Clinton as secretary of state will go down as one of the smartest decisions Obama made after being elected president. After a very intense campaign that was remarkably close, Obama quickly was able to put aside any differences and realize that for the good of the country and the world, the best person for secretary of state was Hillary. The two have surprised nearly everyone by forming a close partnership, and he has given her tremendous latitude in her position as head of the State Department.

Secretary Clinton's favorability rating stands at 65 percent, the highest mark that the former first lady has ever reached in the twenty years that the *Washington Post*–ABC News poll has asked the question. Only 27 percent are unfavorable to her.[177] She is enjoying her tenth straight year as the Gallup Poll's most admired woman.[178]

Secretary Clinton emphasizes the use of what she calls "smart power," or the use of "diplomacy and development alongside defense." Since her arrival Clinton has chosen to employ a pragmatic and tactful handling in all her efforts at State. She has been able to subtly orchestrate some of America's greatest diplomatic successes in the last few years, from forming a broad coalition to stop Qaddafi's massacres in Libya to convincing China and Russia to help isolate Iran and North Korea.

In June 2012, Secretary of State Hillary Clinton made history, visiting her one-hundredth country as America's top diplomat, the most of any secretary of state. During her three-and-a-half-year tenure, Clinton has made seventy trips, spending 337 days on the road and the equivalent of more than 73 days on a plane, according to the State Department. On a recent trip she visited three countries in less than twenty-four hours. She's been everywhere from Afghanistan to Zambia, and that doesn't include an additional twenty-two countries she visited prior to becoming secretary that she has yet to visit in her formal capacity.[179]

No wonder the Senate confirmed her nomination by a vote of 94 to 2.

Though she has said she'll retire as secretary of state and leave public service at the end of Obama's first term, speculation—and hope—that she might seek the presidency again in 2016 remains rampant.

REASON 38

BALANCE AGAINST CONGRESS

BALANCE AGAINST CONGRESS

Most pundits predict that the House of Representatives will remain in the hands of the Republicans after the November elections. My hope is that the Senate will stay under Democratic control, but that's far from certain. It is possible that, come next January, Republicans could be the majority in both houses of the 113th Congress. And with a Republican president, that would spell disaster for the country.

Let's remember the last time the nation had a Republican president and the Republicans controlled both houses of Congress, from 2003 to 2007 (the 108th and 109th Congresses).

What happened?

- Iraq war began
- Tax cuts for millionaires
- Out-of-control spending
- Explosion of the deficit—it more than doubled the first year
- National debt skyrocketed 33 percent
- Failure to respond to Hurricane Katrina
- Failure of immigration reform
- Attempt to classify illegal immigrants and anyone who helped them remain in United States as felons[180]
- Terry Schiavo debacle
- Multiple corruption scandals—Tom DeLay, Bob Ney, Randy "Duke" Cunningham, and Jack Abramoff, to name a few
- 108th Congress: First time in American history that the government cut taxes as it went to war
- 109th Congress: Met for only 242 days, fewest since World War II (less than "Do Nothing" 80th Congress)

The net result? A war completely funded by borrowing, with U.S. debt soaring from $6.4 trillion in March 2003 to $10 trillion in 2008, before the financial crisis. According to Columbia University's Joseph E. Stiglitz and Harvard University's Linda J. Bilmes, two of America's most prominent economists, the true cost of the Iraq War so far is $3 trillion alone.[181] Add to that the Bush-era tax cuts, which reduced revenues by about $1.8 trillion between 2002 and 2009, and you start to see how we got into such an economic mess in the first place.[182]

So the last time the Republicans had both houses of Congress and the presidency we got an irresponsible Congress that gave us huge tax cuts for the rich that we couldn't afford and an unfunded war we shouldn't have fought, setting us up for an economic catastrophe we didn't need.

Is there any doubt we need President Obama?

REASON 39

MICHELLE

I would not be standing here tonight without the unyielding support of my best friend for the last sixteen years . . . the rock of our family, the love of my life, the nation's next first lady . . . Michelle Obama.

—President-elect Barack Obama,
election night, November 4, 2008[183]

Michelle Obama burst on the national scene four years ago, and, like her husband, quickly captured the imagination of the nation. Some say she is her husband's best asset. She is more popular than the president, with a favorability rating of 66 percent, unchanged from two years ago.[184]

As first lady, Michelle Obama has focused her efforts on fighting childhood obesity and improving nutrition. In February 2010, she launched Let's Move!, a comprehensive initiative dedicated to solving childhood obesity, in significant part through improving nutrition education and access to good food, within a generation.

Let's Move! recognizes that everyone has a role to play in reducing childhood obesity. The program brings together parents, caregivers, faith- and community-based organizations, business leaders, teachers and school administrators, doctors, nurses, and government leaders in a nationwide effort to

- create a healthy start for children;
- empower parents and caregivers;
- provide healthy food in schools;
- improve access to healthy, affordable foods;
- encourage kids to be more physically active.

Last year Michelle teamed up with Dr. Jill Biden, Vice President Biden's wife and a professional educator, to launch Joining Forces, a nationwide campaign that encourages all sectors of society to give our service members and their families the opportunities and support they have earned. Joining Forces works closely with American companies committed to answering President Obama's challenge to hire or train one hundred thousand unemployed veterans and military spouses by 2013.

Through innovative programs and initiatives, Joining Forces

- educates the public about the unique needs and strength of America's military families;
- highlights the skills, experience, and dedication of

America's veterans and military spouses to enhance our communities;

- encourages businesses to hire veterans and their spouses;
- expands education, job training, and career development opportunities for veterans and their spouses;
- helps employers create military family–friendly workplaces;
- expands access to wellness programs and resources for military spouses and families;
- helps schools become more responsive to the unique needs of military children and families;
- strengthens connections between the American public and the military.

In addition to her work fighting childhood obesity and supporting military families, First Lady Michelle Obama is active in encouraging national service, promoting the arts and arts education, and speaking out on the importance of balancing career and family.

Accessible, approachable, and stylish, she is an unpretentious and down-to-earth role model for minority women around the globe and someone that many women say they can relate to easily. She was raised in a blue-collar family, once made more money than her husband, and has conquered many obstacles, including racism, as she has become an international sensation.

Michelle is so popular that some people have suggested that she should run for president, like Hillary Clinton did after her husband left office. "Absolutely not. No," she said to laughter, after being asked by a young participant at the White House's annual Take Our Daughters and Sons to Work Day whether she'd want to be president. "I think one of the things you learn about yourself as you get older are what are your strengths and what are your interests. And for me it's other stuff that is not being the president."[185]

Michelle Obama: class, style, smarts, grace, humor, enthusiasm . . . Exactly what you want in a first lady!

REASON 40

THE DUDE CAN SHOOT HOOPS

Shootin' Hoops

There is little doubt that Barack Obama is definitely the hoopster in chief.

From pickup games with LeBron James, Carmelo Anthony and Dwyane Wade, to that amazing three-point jumper he made on the first try with the troops in Kuwait,[186] his passion for basketball is legendary. By no means the tallest president (Barack Obama, at six feet one inch, is shorter than Abe Lincoln, LBJ, and Bill Clinton), no president can match his love of hoops.

In a *Washington Post* introduction to an excerpt from his recent biography, David Maraniss writes:

> To say that President Obama loves basketball understates the role of the sport in his life. He has been devoted to the game for 40 years now, ever since the father he did not know and never saw again gave him his first ball during a brief Christmastime visit. Basketball is central to his self identity. It is global yet American-born, much like him. It is where he found a place of comfort, a family, a mode of expression, a connection from his past to his future. With foundation roots in the Kansas of his white forebears, basketball was also the city game, helping him find his way toward blackness, his introduction to an African American culture that was distant to him when he was young yet his by birthright.[187]

He once wrote in the yearbook of an older high school classmate who wanted to be a lawyer:

> Anyway, been great knowing you and I hope we keep in touch. Good luck in everything you do, and get that law degree. Some day when I am an all-pro basketballer, and I want to sue my team for more money, I'll call on you. Barry.[188]

He loves nothing more than to take a quick break and shoot hoops on the White House basketball court. The sports network ESPN has even picked up on Obama's basketball love, running a segment every year since his election entitled, "Barack-etology," for which the president makes his picks for the men's and women's NCAA basketball tournament.[189] He's pretty good at picking his bracket, consistently ranking in the top percentiles.

He's also a huge fan of the NBA, and was not pleased during the 2011 lockout. "We need our basketball," he remarked at the time.[190]

As he assembled his new administration after the 2008 election, Obama joked that he had put together "the best basketball-playing Cabinet in American history."[191]

He wasn't joking. Take a look:

Arne Duncan
Secretary of Education

Six-feet-five-inch cocaptain at Harvard in the mid-eighties; played in the United States Basketball League and Australia's National Basketball League; and has won three Hoop It Up 3-On-3 titles.

Eric Holder
Attorney General

Six-feet-two-inch cocaptain of the Stuyvesant High Hoopsters in Manhattan; played on Columbia University's freshman team.

James Jones
Retired General; National Security Advisor

In 1963–65, the future Supreme Allied Commander Europe was a six-feet-five-inch front-court reserve at Georgetown University.

Susan Rice
Ambassador to the United Nations

Five-feet-three-inch point guard at National Cathedral School in Washington, D.C., she played for Oxford University when she was a Rhodes scholar.

Timothy Geithner
Treasury Secretary

Though only about five-feet-three-inches, he played on the Federal Reserve Bank of New York league while serving as its president.

For all you Obama fans worried about his chances this fall, the president has one message. As he told the *Sporting News* (October 12, 2011):

"I'm a fourth-quarter player. . . . I don't miss my shots in the fourth quarter."

REASON 41

MALIA AND SASHA

Let's face it folks, Sasha and Malia are adorable.

There's just something about young kids in the White House: JFK Jr. and Caroline, Amy, Chelsea . . .

(Hey, why don't Republican presidents have young kids?)

Smiles, laughs, innocence, adolescence—all these things serve as gentle reminders that the decisions that are made day in and day out in the White House have real consequences, sometimes for generations.

Children help keep things in perspective and remind us of what's really important. They ensure we stay young at heart, even if they make us go gray. And they definitely make sure we don't take ourselves too seriously, even if you are the president of the United States.

Children help keep us keep grounded, and serve as Mother Nature's reality check.

"Voters like a family man in a President," says Fordham University Prof. Monika McDermott. "There's a strength there, but also a softness that is appealing. People like hearing about [Obama's] family and seeing him with his family," McDermott added. "It's a very warming, human aspect."[192]

Like all children, Sasha, eleven, and Malia, fourteen (born on the Fourth of July!), influence their parents and open their eyes to a new generation's perspective and outlook on the world, something from which Barack and Michelle are not immune. President Obama even made reference to this fact when he spoke out in favor of the freedom to marry for gays and lesbians, saying:

> Malia and Sasha—they've got friends whose parents are same-sex couples. And there have been times where

Michelle and I have been sitting around the dinner table. And we've been talking about their friends and their parents. And it . . . wouldn't dawn on [Malia and Sasha] that somehow their friends' parents would be treated differently. It doesn't make sense to them. And frankly, that's the kind of thing that prompts a change of perspective: not wanting to somehow explain to your child why somebody should be treated differently when it comes to the eyes of the law.

—President Barack Obama,
Robin Roberts ABC News Interview[193]

Malia and Sasha make President Obama the tenth consecutive U.S. president who has been the father of at least one daughter. Romney has no daughters. Why buck the trend? ;-)

REASON 42

THE GUY CAN SING

By now, President Obama's few bars of the Al Green classic "Let's Stay Together," which he sang at a January 2012 fundraiser at the Apollo Theater in Harlem, are the stuff of presidential legend.[194] The Associated Press YouTube video of his performance has had over 2.5 million hits.[195] In the days following the event, digital download sales for Green's song jumped 490 percent. Talk about a stimulus plan![196]

But that is not Obama's only crooning performance, not by a long shot.

Turns out he created several singing sensations well before he became president.

Back in June 2006, he busted out a smooth eight-second baritone of Dionne Warwick's "Walk on By" during an appearance at a high school in East Orange, New Jersey. Reminiscing about when he and his friends were young and wanted to "like, really be smooth . . . you slip in the Dionne Warwick," he advised the young men in the audience.[197]

After thanking Aretha Franklin at a 2008 Labor Day rally in Detroit, he broke out a soulful rasp of "Chain of Fools."[198]

Then, two years later, as president, Obama and family joined Sir Paul McCartney, Elvis Costello, and a host of others at the White House for a rendition of one of pop music's most timeless classics: "Hey Jude."[199]

And earlier this year, he sang parts of the blues anthem of his hometown, "Sweet Home Chicago," at a White House Event with B. B. King and Mick Jagger.[200]

The president is also known to dance occasionally: he danced to "Crazy in Love" on *The Ellen DeGeneres Show*.[201]

Not to be outdone, First Lady Michelle Obama was caught dancing the "Dougie" at a middle school event as part of her Let's Move Campaign.[202]

I wonder what number he'll belt out at the inaugural ball next year?

REASON 43

HIS HUGE SMILE

SMILE!

Every time I see that smile I can't help but, well, smile!

Barack Obama's smile is electrifying, magnetic, contagious. When he flashes that toothy grin, you can't help but feel good and smile back, like he's your friend. You almost want to give him a wave, like someone you might see on the street and say hello to.

Dentists are beside themselves. Here are a few comments from a survey conducted by *TheWealthyDentist.com*:

> I think as Commander in Chief a great smile is important, because you are constantly in the public eye. Your smile should be cosmetically pleasing for image, a boost for dentistry as a whole, and an invaluable tool in building rapport for communication to America and the world. (Georgia dentist)

> Barack Obama has a beautiful smile. He is just blessed with good genetics. His teeth appear to be aligned in an almost ideal Angles Class I occlusion. From a dental esthetic standpoint, the other presidential candidates don't have a chance. (Illinois dentist)[203]

There's no question that we, as humans, are drawn to people with happy, friendly faces. The smile is reassuring and inviting, and inspires confidence and trust. Obama's grin is genuine, effortless, not at all like those forced smiles politicians so often wear. His smile, among other attributes, has undoubtedly helped drive his likability and favorability, huge assets at a time when politics can be so negative, dark, and confrontational.

Science has actually shown that the human brain prefers happy faces and can recognize them more quickly than negative expressions. Deborah Blum writes in *Psychology Today*: "Smiles are such an important part of communication that we see them far more clearly than any other expression." According to Blum, research shows that "we can pick up a smile at 300 feet—the length of a football field." She calls the smile "the most recognizable human signal in the world."[204]

Like his commitment to America, his faith in this country, and his passion for basketball, Barack Obama's smile never wavers, literally. Eric Spiegelman, a blogger, was scanning the State Department's Flickr page and noticed that, despite posing for over one hundred photographs with foreign leaders for the 2009 UN General Assembly opening, his smile never changed. Check out the video he made: http://vimeo.com/6747788.

Even superstar Cher has gushed over Obama's grin, tweeting just before meeting him, "Cant wait 2 c beautiful smile in person."[205]

MSNBC's Chris Matthews has said that Obama's smile is worth five to ten points on Election Day. I'm not sure it's worth quite that much, but given how close this election is likely to be, I'll take even a point or two.

REASON 44

HE DRIVES THE RIGHT CRAZY

C'mon folks, you know you love it.... Obama drives the Right crazy!

I'd thought I'd seen it all after working for Bill Clinton, who on the day of his impeachment by the House had the highest favorability rating of his presidency. But that was nothing.

For a while it was Hillary who, it seemed, just by her very presence could send the right wing screaming through the streets. Though she did win some Republican praise with her strong performance in the Senate, all that was forgotten when she began her race for the White House.

But as they say, be careful what you wish for, because as soon as Obama became competitive with Hillary, the right wing's collective head exploded.

Who was this guy, with the "radical, socialist agenda" and an uncanny ability to move millions just by opening his mouth? How dare he upset our plans to continue to amass great wealth for the very few and distribute the rest according to how we see fit? This is our mess, they cried. Don't come in here and try to fix it (you'll see how bad we really screwed it up!).

Health care, for everyone? You can't be serious! Opportunity for all, including immigrants? No way! More oversight and transparency on how we conduct our business? Outrageous! Clean energy? Aaaaahhhh!!! Quick, grab the garlic!!!

Sure, there's a very troubling dark side to some of this among an unfortunate minority. Yes, I'm talking about the racists, those ignorant, unfortunate individuals who object to Obama first and foremost because he is black. And I know they are out there, but I do believe, perhaps thanks to my better angels, that they represent a dwindling minority.

Calls for Obama's impeachment over health care, immigration, his birth certificate, and Libya, among other reasons, abound. Of course, there are some bright spots amid all this craziness and hyperbole. The theater displayed on television and across the airwaves can be downright comical. The flustering, blustering, bloviating blowhards can make for really great comedy. One commentator, Rush Limbaugh, even pledged that he would move to Costa Rica if health reform passed. Maybe he was attracted by that country's socialized health care system, and that its citizens have a life expectancy second only to Canada in the western hemisphere. Well, despite passage of the law, and the Supreme Court's constitutional validation, we (unfortunately) see no signs of his bags being packed.

Hey right-wing wing nuts, did you know that Obama is also tough on defense, cuts taxes for the middle class, and supports charter schools?

REASON 45

OUR DOGS WILL BE SAFE

OUR DOGS WILL BE SAFE

Perhaps no other reason to vote for Obama is more important than this one, according to my basset hound, Rusty. We have had many long chats about this topic, while he lies on the couch (wait, what are you doing on the couch!) and I outline my rationales for the president's reelection. "But what about the dogs?" Rusty howls. "What about us?" He's petrified.

And with good reason. By now, everybody knows the story. Mitt Romney, during a family vacation, strapped his dog, Seamus, to the roof of his car during a twelve-hour drive to Canada. The Irish setter got sick during the ride on top of a faux-wood paneled station wagon. Mittens stopped the car, cleaned up the dog, strapped him back up on top, and kept moving.

"Dogs Aren't Luggage" T-shirts and bumper stickers are everywhere. "Dogs Against Romney" has over sixty thousand likes on Facebook and a Web site, complete with buttons and magnets. They've even formed a Dogs Against Romney super PAC and organized a sister division, Horses Against Romney. Animal rights activists protested outside the Westminster dog show in February.

Even a rival Republican strategist remarked, "Quite frankly, I'm not sure I'm going to listen to the value judgment of a guy who strapped his dog to the top of the roof of his car and went hurling down the highway."[206]

Rusty has already organized the Manhattan chapter of "Dogs for Obama," which meets weekly at the Washington Square dog park in the West Village. He's even organized a Bone-Raiser and extended an invitation to Bo, the First Dog, who he hopes will be the main barker for the event.

"You know, I'm not going to take this lying down," Rusty barks. Yeah right.

REASON 46

MY BARBER TOLD ME TO

Women have known this secret for years: Listen to the person who cuts your hair . . . they know everything. They've seen it all, and more importantly, they've heard it all. I don't know what it is about that chair, but people settle in and the advice just starts flowing. The street smarts and intuition that hairdressers have is uncanny—and unlike most any other profession in the world.

It's about time men learned this lesson. My barber, Humberto, has been around the block a few times. He's an immigrant from Cuba who came over on a raft during the Mariel boat lift in 1980, a refugee from Castro's oppressive regime. He made his way up from Miami to New York a generation ago and has no desire to return to Little Havana. "It's too hot," he says. And why should he? He's got an enormous following of loyal customers. When his old barbershop closed, and he moved down the street to a new location, they painted "Humberto Is Here!" with an arrow pointing to the new store.

Humberto speaks with the quiet confidence of a man who has struggled, learned much along the way, and wants to impart this knowledge to his clients. He talks in hushed tones, and I sometimes struggle to hear him above the buzzing sound of the clippers. We'll talk about the weather or his cat and occasionally chat about some of the regulars who frequent his shop. But every so often he'll stop cutting, put down his scissors, lower his voice even further, and say, "You know, Bernard . . . " That's when I know to really pay attention.

The other day, while I was sitting in his chair and looking at the many photographs adorning his mirror, suddenly he stops snipping. "Bernard," he says. "Yes," I reply, immediately snapping to attention, not wanting to miss a pearl of wisdom that he might impart to me this day. "You're voting for Obama, right," posed not so much as a question but more like an admonition you might hear coming out of the mouth of Nucky Thompson, Steve Buscemi's character on *Boardwalk Empire*. "'Cause, I don't know about this other guy."

"Of course I am, Humberto," I replied quickly. "Good," he said, picking up the scissors again. "I'm glad to hear that."

As I left ten minutes later, I checked out my new 'do in the mirror. "Wow, this is the best cut I've had in ages," I thought. "Good thing I'm voting for Obama!"

REASON 47

I'M A DEMOCRAT

OK, I admit it. I'm a partisan. One hundred percent Democrat, through and through. I've only voted for one Republican my whole life—Rudy Giuliani for mayor of New York, the second time around. And boy did I live to regret it! I'm not making that mistake again. I bleed blue, and I love donkeys. Obama, I'm yours.

But it wasn't always this way. Back when I was a little kid, I was a Republican, like my father. From the time I was five years old, I was obsessed with politics, and with Richard Nixon. I remember my dad going to the '72 inauguration; I wanted to go so badly. I must have flipped through that little blue program he brought back a hundred times.

Fast-forward to 1976. I had a big poster of Gerald Ford hanging on my bedroom door. I was ten years old. Sitting on the floor beside my folks, I kept track of the delegate counts during the state-by-state roll call as I watched both conventions. I remember the brief excitement in the hall when it was rumored that Reagan would be on the ticket.

Then suddenly, everything changed. It was January 20, 1977, Inauguration Day, and we watched from a balcony as President Jimmy Carter walked down Pennsylvania Avenue that crisp winter afternoon. In that moment, everything started to make sense. My political consciousness was born. I remember arguing politics with my great-uncle Sam a year or two later. "Bernie," he said. "Just wait till you get older; then you'll become a Republican." Sorry Uncle Sam, not a chance.

I found growing up as a teenager under Ronald Reagan oppressive. At seventeen I ran as a Gary Hart delegate, and went on to manage a big volunteer operation for Walter Mondale during my first semester at Brown. I was so naïve I thought he actually might pull off an upset. Courtesy of a classmate whose father was running for president, I spent winter break of my senior year in Council Bluffs, Iowa. Five months later I started working full-time for the Dukakis campaign. When Bush won later that year, I kept my promise to leave the country, and signed up for the Peace Corps, serving for two years in Senegal.

When I returned, in the summer of '91, I had already decided to support Bill Clinton, a little-known governor who I had heard speak (for a long time, I might add) at the 1988 Democratic convention. I was fortunate enough to work for him from just after the fall of Congress in 1994 through the end of his term, as well as on Hillary Clinton's first run for the Senate in 2000 and the early part of Gore's presidential campaign. An ardent Hillary supporter, I took to the airwaves in 2008 to argue her case, and when Obama triumphed, I quickly took up his cause and have been advocating for him ever since.

Somewhere along the way I even managed to convince my father to switch sides, at least most of the time. Now I've just got to work on my son.

REASON 48

HE'S COOL

One of the biggest problems for Mitt Romney is his inability to relate to the common man. People look at Romney and see an uptight rich guy. He seems wooden, stiff, patrician. Must be all that blue blood circulating inside of him. He lacks emotion and often appears disconnected, like he's beaming in from some other planet.

Barack Obama, on the other hand, is the epitome of cool. He oozes smoothness. He's laid-back, hip, easygoing, chill. He's the guy you want to hang out and shoot some hoops with, or maybe just have a beer. Honestly, can you name another head of state as cool as Barack Obama? Obama's the cool dude in school you brag to your friends about.

Since becoming a global sensation in 2008, his coolness factor has only gotten hotter. This past April, his "Slow Jam the News" segment on Jimmy Fallon's late-night comedy show took the Internet by storm. President Obama is so cool that sometimes he doesn't even have to do anything to be cool. In the summer of 2010, cult bloggers speculated that Obama was in the 1993 video for Tag Team's single "Whoomp (There It Is)." The guy looked enough like the president, and it's not that outrageous to suggest that a guy as cool as Obama would have made a cameo in a 1990s' hip-hop video.[207]

From modest beginnings in Hawaii, Obama wasn't born with a silver spoon in his mouth like Romney. He complains about his student loans and enjoys visiting local bars and eateries when on the road. While there, he hangs out like a regular guy, ordering take-out and raising a pint with pals. But he's just as comfortable hanging with friends and supporters such as George Clooney, Brad Pitt, Angelina Jolie, and Lady Gaga. He looks awesome in a pair of dark shades. And the guy can croon a tune like nobody's business.

Contrast that with Mitt Romney. Every time Romney opens his mouth, his stilted manner of speaking makes him seem out of touch. His constant use of "gosh," "golly," and "gee" make him sound like he is from a different time. John McWhorter, writing recently in *The New Republic*, notes, "[T]here are few better ways to connote the air of a mannequin in 2012 than by saying gosh with a straight face."[208]

The GOP is so afraid of Obama's coolness factor that Karl Rove's super PAC, American Crossroads, put out an ad attacking Obama for being too cool. McCain tried the same thing in 2008, when his campaign attacked Obama for being "the biggest celebrity in the world." How'd that work out for ya, John?

Truth is, in America, cool wins out every time. Golly gee, we just can't seem to help ourselves.

REASON 49

SECOND TERMS ARE NEVER KIND TO PRESIDENTS (FOR MY REPUBLICAN FRIENDS)

So you're reading this book thinking to yourself, "There's no way I'm going to vote for Obama." Maybe you're a hard-core conservative, or perhaps you really disagree with his policies, or maybe you just don't like the guy. Well, my friends on the right, here's a reason to reconsider. History shows that the second time around for most presidents is usually fraught with peril, and sometimes they are just downright disasters.

A total of fifteen presidents out of forty-four have been reelected so far, and not one had a second term that was better than his first, according to presidential historian Robert Dallek. In fact, for half, the second term was "catastrophic," according to *USA Today*'s Susan Page.[209]

Let's take a quick look:

- George Washington faced the Whiskey Rebellion.
- Thomas Jefferson enacted a disastrous embargo that nearly tanked the economy.
- James Madison fled Washington as the Brits burned down the White House.
- Andrew Jackson forced the widespread removal of Native Americans.
- Ulysses S. Grant suffered scandal after scandal.
- Grover Cleveland dealt with a severe economic depression.
- Woodrow Wilson saw his League of Nations rebuffed.
- Franklin Roosevelt tried to pack the Supreme Court.
- Dwight Eisenhower weathered Sputnik and the U-2 incident.
- Richard Nixon resigned.
- Ronald Reagan sold arms for hostages.
- Bill Clinton was impeached.
- George W. Bush caused an economic meltdown.

Truman and Johnson, who came into office following the deaths of FDR and Kennedy, had such bad second terms that neither man chose to stand for reelection.

USA Today's Susan Page notes that political scientist Colleen Shogan of Virginia's George Mason University studied legislative successes in the first and second terms of Reagan and Clinton. Shogan concluded, "Power dissipates over time, and opportunities for legislative reform diminish." In Shogan's study of major campaign promises, Page reports, Reagan's success rate of 100 percent during his first term fell to 25 percent in his second, while Clinton's 87 percent achievement rating in his first term dropped to 38 percent in round two.[210]

You don't want Obama to succeed? Then just vote to reelect him!

REASON 50

REPUBLICANS WILL HAVE A LOCK ON CONGRESS IN 2014 (ANOTHER ONE FOR THE REPUBLICANS AMONG US)

REPUBLICANS' LOCK ON CONGRESS

OK, my elephant-loving friends. Don't like Obama but not crazy about Romney? (Sounds like about half the GOP electorate.) Here's a reason to vote for Obama that you can really sink your teeth into.

The incumbent president's party almost always loses seats in the midterm elections, especially the second time around. Some even call it "The Sixth-Year Curse."[211] Since 1862 the president's party has averaged losses of about thirty-two seats in the House and more than two seats in the Senate during the midterm elections. Bill Clinton was the first president since the Civil War to survive a sixth-year election without such an electoral catastrophe.[212]

Remember 2006? The Democrats captured the House, the Senate, and a majority of governorships and state legislatures from the Republicans, in a sweeping rebuke to the GOP amid plummeting poll numbers for George W. Bush. The Democratic tidal wave brought Speaker Nancy Pelosi to power and paved the way for the passage of health care reform a few short years later.

Then fast-forward to 2010, Obama's first midterms. The result? An astounding victory for the Republicans. Democrats lost 63 seats in the House that year, in the largest seat change since 1948, and the largest for any midterm election since 1938. Out with Nancy Pelosi, in with John Boehner. The GOP also gained 6 seats in the Senate and 680 seats in state legislative races, breaking the previous record of 628 won by the Democrats in the aftermath of Watergate in 1974. Republicans took control of twenty-nine of the nation's fifty governorships.

Sure, you'll have to suffer the indignity of Obama's reelection. But just imagine your excitement as 2014 draws near. How many seats will the Democrats lose? Seventy? Maybe even seventy-five, more than Roosevelt lost in 1938? You'll be able to crush his legislative agenda, tie him up in knots! Oooooohhhhh, picture the gridlock, the humiliation . . . and the opportunities for 2016!

So go ahead, my right-leaning, Romney-wary friends, hold your nose and vote for Obama. Think how much you'll have to celebrate in only a couple of years!

REASON 51

YOU KNOW WHERE HE STANDS

Voters should have a chance to choose between clear alternatives. Obama—consistent with his obligations as president—has laid out a multiyear budget embodying his vision for the future, and it has been evaluated by independent experts. It is time for Romney to do the same.

—former Treasury secretary Lawrence Summers [213]

President Obama has laid out a clear plan and vision for America if he is reelected. Romney's agenda remains vague, uncertain, and full of holes. And no wonder: Romney has flip-flopped on so many critical issues, it is unsurprising he cannot lay out his core beliefs. To win over the radical right, he has changed his position so many times on so many different issues that he may have lost his core beliefs . . . and that is a frightening statement to ponder.

In February, Obama released his budget for America: Reduce deficits by more than $4 trillion over the next decade, bring federal discretionary spending to its lowest levels since the 1960s, $2.50 in spending cuts for every $1 in additional revenue, everyone pays his or her fair share of taxes, repeal the Bush tax cuts for families making more than $250,000 a year, and close loopholes and shelters for the rich.[214]

The independent Congressional Budget Office confirmed that Obama's plan would stabilize the debt as a share of the economy, putting us back on solid fiscal ground. And it would accomplish these goals while making targeted investments in education, research, and infrastructure that are essential to strengthening and growing our economy for the future.

Mitt Romney has yet to explain how he can possibly cut taxes by $5 trillion and lower the deficit while dramatically increasing spending on defense. Frankly, it's just not mathematically possible. And he knows it. That's why Romney is notoriously circumspect in giving details regarding which programs he would cut, telling Stephen Hayes, a senior writer at the conservative *Weekly Standard*:

> One of the things I found in a short campaign against Ted Kennedy was that when I said, for instance, that I wanted to eliminate the Department of Education, that was used to suggest I don't care about education. So I think it's important for me to point out that I anticipate that there will be departments and agencies that will either be eliminated or combined with other agencies. . . . So will there be some that get eliminated or combined? The answer is yes, but I'm not going to give you a list right now.

Hayes then noted, "In a conversation with him, you can feel him thinking about his words, trying to make sure he doesn't say anything that could become the latest in a string of gaffes. . . . His inveterate risk-aversion often comes off as a lack of commitment to conservative policies and goals."[215]

Barack Obama, on the other hand, has clearly demonstrated his consistent commitment to certain principles and ideals and has taken decisive stands, even when they may not be politically advantageous. Pushing health care reform in his first year, bailing out GM and Chrysler, and supporting the freedom to marry for same-sex couples are just a few examples.

Obama is running on his record—a record of concrete steps he has undertaken along with specific proposals for action he will take in his next term. Obama has successfully passed a detailed vision for improving the health care system. Romney promises to repeal it but gives only a vague idea of what he would replace it with. Obama had to make the tough choices that averted another Great Depression. Romney has been able to play it safe, criticizing from the sidelines as he's run for president these last eight years.

Romney's record as a flip-flopper is well-known. His likely policies as president are not.

Obama's record—like it or not—is out there for all the world to see. You know where he stands.

Judge away, America.

REASON 52

AMERICA HAS REGAINED ITS GLOBAL PRESTIGE

GLOBAL PRESTIGE

Barack Obama acted quickly to repair America's reputation abroad, traveling to twenty-one foreign countries during his first year in office, shattering the previous records of fifteen held by George H. W. Bush and Gerald Ford.

His efforts to strengthen alliances and international partnerships and to promote democracy, free trade, and the rule of law in a globally interconnected world have helped to rebuild international support for the United States and restore the American brand abroad.

His proactive efforts to win friends and influence people around the globe stand in stark contrast to the failed unilateralist approach of George W. Bush, whose cowboy style turned off much of the world. Obama was awarded the Nobel Peace Prize for his efforts, particularly in arms control, less than nine months after taking office. President Nicolas Sarkozy of France said at the time that the award signaled "America's return to the hearts of the world's peoples," while Chancellor Angela Merkel of Germany remarked, "In a short time he has been able to set a new tone throughout the world and to create a readiness for dialogue."[216]

There is clear empirical evidence that President Obama has greatly enhanced the American brand overseas. A 2010 BBC World Service poll of nearly thirty thousand people found that more people abroad viewed America as a positive force than a negative one. CBS News reported that "the U.S. is seen as having a positive influence in twenty of twenty-eight countries; an average of 46 percent view the country as a positive influence, while 34 percent see it as a negative influence.[217] "After a year, it appears the 'Obama effect' is real," declared Steven Kull, one of the study directors.[218] This was the first time in the five-year history of the poll that America was seen as more of a positive influence than a negative one. Negative views of the United States declined by nine points on average, while positive views increased four points. "People around the world today view the United States more positively than at any time since the second Iraq war," said pollster Doug Miller, whose firm, GlobeScan, conducted the survey.[219]

A more recent study of over twenty-five thousand people across twenty-one countries conducted in Spring 2012 by the Pew Research Center's Global Attitudes Project confirms that Europeans and Japanese remain largely confident in President Obama. According to the 2012 Pew Global Attitudes Survey, Obama consistently receives higher ratings than President Bush, especially in Western Europe and Japan, but also in several predominantly Muslim nations. "Roughly nine-in-ten in France (92%) and Germany (89%) would like to see him re-elected," the report states, "as would large majorities in Britain (73%), Spain (71%), Italy (69%), and the Czech Republic (67%). Most Brazilians (72%) and Japanese (66%) agree." The survey also finds that majorities or pluralities in twelve countries have a favorable view of the United States, while only five nations hold a negative opinion. "Majorities or pluralities in 18 of 20 countries admire the U.S. for its science and technology," the study noted, and "around the world, U.S. ideas about democracy and American ways of doing business have become more popular since Obama took office."[220]

While the world may not agree with some of Obama's policies, there is no question that our allies have great confidence in President Obama's leadership, and that he has repaired America's strong international standing, which was lost under President Bush.

Mitt Romney, who has surrounded himself with the neocon hawks who helped drag us into the Iraq War, seems intent on taking us back to those dark days. His naiveté on national security, combined with his proclivity for short-sighted, overly aggressive pronouncements regarding foreign affairs, could easily strain alliances and cost America dearly, both in terms of prestige and dollars. His comments on Iran, Afghanistan,

Russia, and China have already caused many in the diplomatic world to question his judgment, including former secretary of state Colin Powell, who said, "I think [Romney] needs to not just accept these cataclysmic pronouncements. He needs to really think carefully about these [statements]. . . . Let's not go creating enemies where none need exist . . . let's not hyperbolize the situation."[221] Even outgoing Russian president (and current prime minister) Dmitry Medvedev chided Romney, suggesting that he "check the time—it is now 2012, not the mid-1970s."[222]

Now more than ever, America needs a president who understands that, in a fragile global economy, the economic and security interests of the United States are enhanced when our nation's reputation around the world is strong.

The world depends on America to point the way toward freedom for all citizens and looks to our great nation for the moral leadership and sense of justice that unites the global community and inspires people of all lands to dream of a better life. Barack Obama has spent nearly four years rebuilding the American brand abroad. Let's not let Mitt Romney's ignorance and penchant for exaggeration destroy it.

NOTES

1. Josh Gerstein, "Osama bin Laden Operation, Part 2," *Politico*, Oct. 29, 2012, http://www.politico.com/news/stories/0412/75696.html.

2. 2008 Democratic Party presidential candidate debate, ABC News, Aug. 19, 2007, http://abcnews.go.com/Politics/Decision2008/story?id=3498294&page=3U.

3. President Barack Obama, remarks in Fayetteville, North Carolina, "The World Beyond Iraq," March 19, 2008, http://www.presidency.ucsb.edu/ws/index.php?pid=77035#axzz1yKz5J0to.

4. "The Second Presidential Debate," *New York Times*, October 7, 2008, http://elections.nytimes.com/2008/president/debates/transcripts/second-presidential-debate.html.

5. George W. Bush, Presidential Press Conference, March 13, 2002; http://georgewbush-hitehouse.archives.gov/news/releases/2002/03/20020313-8.html6 George W. Bush, Presidential Press Conference, March 13,,2002; http://georgewbush-whitehouse.archives.gov/news/releases/2002/03/20020313-8.html.

6. John F. Kerry, "Tora Bora Revisited: How We Failed to Get Bin Laden and Why It Matters Today," *Report to the Members of the Committee of Foreign Relations United States Senate*, November 30, 2009, http://www.foreign.senate.gov/imo/media/doc/Tora_Bora_Report.pdf.

7. Faiz Shakir, "Bush Tells Barnes Capturing Bin Laden Is 'Not a Top Priority Use of American Resources,'" Think Progress via Fox News, Sept. 14, 2006, http://thinkprogress.org/politics/2006/09/14/7472/barnes-osama.

8. Liz Sidoti, "Romney defends his shifts on issues," *USA Today*, April 26, 2007, http://www.usatoday.com/news/politics/2007-04-26-972397336_x.htm.

9. Steve Holland, "Romney Attacks Obama Over Pakistan Warning," Reuters, Aug. 4, 2007, http://in.reuters.com/article/2007/08/04/idINIndia-28811520070804.

10. President Barack Obama, speech to the Illinois state legislature, October 2002, http://www.cnn.com/ELECTION/2008/issues/issues.iraq.html.

11. "Direct military leaders to end war in Iraq," *PolitiFact.com*, January 21, 2009, http://www.PolitiFact.com/truth-o-meter/promises/obameter/promise/125/direct-military-leaders-to-end-war-in-iraq.

12. Remarks of President Barack Obama—As Prepared for Delivery: "Responsibly Ending the War in Iraq," White House, February 27, 2009, http://www.whitehouse.gov/the_press_office/Remarks-of-President-Barack-Obama-Responsibly-Ending-the-War-in-Iraq.

13. Mark Lander, "U.S. Troops to Leave Iraq by Year's End, Obama Says," *New York Times*, December 21, 2011, http://www.nytimes.com/2011/10/22/world/middleeast/president-obama-announces-end-of-war-in-iraq.html?pagewanted=all.

14. http://www.iraqbodycount.org/.

15. "Current Employment Statistics Highlights December 2009," Bureau of Labor Statistics, January 8, 2010, http://www.bls.gov/ces/highlights122009.pdf,

16. "We cut taxes for 95 percent of working families," *PolitiFact.com.com* http://www.PolitiFact.com/truth-o-meter/statements/2010/jan/28/barackobama/tax-cut-95-percent-stimulus-made-it-so.

17. Jennifer Cohen, "Recovery.gov Releases Newest ARRA Jobs Numbers," New America Foundation, February 21, 2011, http://edmoney.newamerica.net/blogposts/2011/recoverygov_releases_newest_arra_jobs_numbers-43837.

18. Community Oriented Policing Services (COPS), FY 2012 Budget Request, http://www.justice.gov/jmd/2012summary/pdf/fy12-cops-bud-summary.pdf.

19. Heather Boushey, "MarketWatch Commentary: Conservatives in Congress stymie job gains; Not too late to OK infrastructure spending," *Wall Street Journal*, July 6, 2012, http://articles.marketwatch.com/2012-07-06/commentary/32560563_1_pace-of-job-creation-job-gains-employers.

20. Tom Hamburger, "Romney's Bain Capital invested in companies that moved jobs overseas," June 21, 2012, http://www.washingtonpost.com/business/economy/romneys-bain-capital-invested-in-companies-that-moved-jobs-overseas/2012/06/21/gJQAsD9ptV_story.html.

21. U.S. Department of Commerce, Insourcing American Jobs forum at the White House, January 11, 2012, http://www.commerce.gov/blog/2012/01/11/insourcing-american-jobs-forum-white-house.

22. Executive Office of the President, "The Economic Impact of the American Recovery and Reinvestment Act of 2009," November 18, 2010, http://www.whitehouse.gov/sites/default/files/cea_5th_arra_report.pdf.

23 Compiled from U.S. Bureau of Labor statistics data, http://www.bls.gov/home.htm.
24 Interesting Fact: The Cleveland Plain Dealer calculated that between April 1945 and September 2010, Democrats held the presidency for nearly thirty years and created 54.2 million jobs. Republicans controlled the White House for thirty-six years during that time and created just 34.6 million jobs. Rich Exner, U.S. job growth (and loss) under presidents; Democrats and Republicans," *Plain Dealer*, October 17, 2010, http://www.cleveland.com/datacentral/index.ssf/2010/10/us_job_growth_and_loss_under_p.html.
25 President Barack Obama, speech at Cuyahoga Community College, Sept. 8, 2010, http://www.cleveland.com/open/index.ssf/2010/09/transcript_of_president_obamas_1.html.
26 White House, as published in "Bringing Jobs Back to the United States," *Imperial Valley (California) News*, May 8, 2012, http://imperialvalleynews.com/index.php/news/jobs/510-bringing-jobs-back-to-the-united-states.
27 Press release, Internal Revenue Service, "Payroll Tax Cut Extended to the End of 2012; Revised Payroll," February 23, 2012, http://www.irs.gov/newsroom/article/0,,id=254723,00.html.
28 "401(k) Balances and Changes Due to Market Volatility," Employee Benefit Research Institute, http://www.ebri.org/?fa=401kbalances.
29 U.S. Department of the Treasury, "Making Home Affordable: Program Performance Report Through Apr8l 2012,: http://www.treasury.gov/initiatives/financial-stability/results/MHA-Reports/Documents/April%202012%20MHA%20Report%20WITH%20SERVICER%20ASSESSMENTS_FINAL.pdf.
30 AAA, *Daily Fuel Gauge Report*, as of July 7, 2012, http://fuelgaugereport.aaa.com/?redirectto=http://fuelgaugereport.opisnet.com/index.asp.
31 Lori Montgomery, "President Obama signs six-month extension of emergency unemployment benefits," July 23, 2010, http://www.washingtonpost.com/wp-dyn/content/article/2010/07/22/AR2010072203825.html.
32 President Barack Obama, "Weekly Address: A New Chapter in Afghanistan," the White House Press Office, May 5, 2012, http://www.whitehouse.gov/the-press-office/2012/05/05/weekly-address-new-chapter-afghanistan.
33 National Economic Council, "The Buffet Rule: A Basic Principle of Tax Fairness" April 2011; http://www.whitehouse.gov/sites/default/files/Buffett_Rule_Report_Final.pdf.
34 U.S. Internal Revenue Service, "SOI Tax Stats—Individual Income Tax Returns Publication 1304 (Complete Report)," http://www.irs.gov/taxstats/indtaxstats/article/0,,id=134951,00.html.
35 President Barack Obama, "Remarks by the President on the Economy in Parma, Ohio," Sept. 8, 2010, the White House Press Office, http://www.whitehouse.gov/the-press-office/2010/09/08/remarks-president-economy-parma-ohio.
36 Michael Linden and Michael Ettlinger, "Obama vs. Bush: Who's the Bigger Tax Cutter?" Center for American Progress, Sept. 13, 2011, http://www.americanprogress.org/issues/2011/09/obama_bush_taxes.html.
37 Angie Drobnic Holan, "Tax Cut for 95 Percent? The Stimulus Made It So," *PolitiFact.com*, Jan. 28, 2010, http://www.PolitiFact.com/truth-o-meter/statements/2010/jan/28/barack-obama/tax-cut-95-percent-stimulus-made-it-so.
38 "Bogus Tax Attack Against Obama," *FactCheck.org*, May 17, 2012, http://www.factcheck.org/2012/05/a-bogus-tax-attack-against-obama/.
39 Ezra Klein, "The Bush Tax cuts in one chart," *Washington Post*, December 6, 2010; http://voices.washingtonpost.com/ezra-klein/2010/12/the_bush_tax_cuts_in_one_chart.html
40 President Barack Obama and Vice President Joseph Biden, "Remarks by the President and Vice President at the Signing of the Health Insurance Reform Bill," March 23, 2010, the White House Press Office, http://www.whitehouse.gov/the-press-office/remarks-president-and-vice-president-signing-health-insurance-reform-bill.
41 Centers for Medicare & Medicare Services, "National Health Expenditure Projections 2012–2012," January 2011, p. 1, http://www.cms.gov/Research-Statistics-Data-and-Systems/Statistics-Trends-and-Reports/NationalHealthExpendData/downloads/proj2010.pdf.
42 Jessica Dickler, "Family Healthcare to Exceed 20,000 This Year," CNN, March 29, 2012, http://money.cnn.com/2012/03/29/pf/healthcare-costs/index.htm.
43 Josh Levs, "What the health care ruling means to you," CNN, June 28, 2012, http://www.cnn.com/2012/06/28/politics/supreme-court-health-effects/index.html.
44 Melody Barnes, "Health Care Reform Act Must Not be Lost," CNN, March 29, 2012, http://www.cnn.com/2012/03/29/opinion/barnes-health-care-reform/index.html.
45 "The 80/20 Rule: Providing Value and Rebates to Millions of Consumers," *HealthCare.gov*, June 21, 2012, http://www.healthcare.gov/law/resources/reports/mlr-rebates06212012a.html.

46. Douglas W. Elmendorf, "CBO's Analysis of the Major Health Care Legislation Enacted in March 2010," Congressional Budget Office testimony, March 30, 2011, http://www.cbo.gov/sites/default/files/cbofiles/ftpdocs/121xx/doc12119/03-30-healthcarelegislation.pdf.
47. Jesse Lee, "President Obama Signs Small Business Jobs Act—Learn What's In It," the White House Blog, Sept. 27, 2010, http://www.whitehouse.gov/blog/2010/09/27/president-obama-signs-small-business-jobs-act-learn-whats-it.
48. National Economic Council, "The Small Business Agenda, Growing America's Small Businesses to Win the Future," May 2011, p. 12, http://www.sba.gov/sites/default/files/Small%20Business%20Agenda%20NEC.pdf.
49. U.S. Department of the Treasury, "Overview of Small Business Lending Fund," http://www.treasury.gov/resource-center/sb-programs/Documents/SBLF_Fact_Sheet_Final.pdf.
50. U.S. Small Business Administration, "Small Business Jobs Act of 2010," http://www.sba.gov/content/small-business-jobs-act-2010.
51. Center on Budget and Policy Priorities, "Chart Book: The Legacy of the Great Recession," July 6. 2012, http://www.cbpp.org/cms/index.cfm?fa=view&id=3252; Truth-O-Meter, "Half-Truth: Debbie Wasserman Schultz says Obama has created 'millions' of manufacturing jobs," *PolitiFact.com*, http://www.politifact.com/truth-o-meter/statements/2011/nov/15/debbie-wasserman-schultz/debbie-wasserman-schultz-says-obama-has-created-mi/ http://www.bushtoll.com/wp-content/uploads/2012/03/BLS-job-stats-report-1939-2012.pdf
52. S. Mitra Kalita, "Americans see 18% of Wealth Vanish," *Wall Street Journal*, March 13 2009, http://online.wsj.com/article/SB123687371369308675.html.
53. Alan S. Blinder and Mark Zandi, "How the Great Recession was Brought to an End," July 27, 2010, pp. 1, 6, http://www.economy.com/mark-zandi/documents/End-of-Great-Recession.pdf.
54. U.S. Department of the Treasury, *The Financial Response in Charts*, April 2012, p. 9, http://www.treasury.gov/resource-center/data-chart-center/Documents/20120413_FinancialCrisisResponse.pdf.
55. David Roeder, "Geithner in Chicago: Obama 'Prevented' a Depression," *Post-Tribune*, April 4, 2012, http://posttrib.suntimes.com/business/11710197-420/geithner-in-chicago-obama-prevented-a-depression.html.
56. Mitt Romney, "Let Detroit Go Bankrupt," *New York Times*, Nov. 18, 2008, http://www.nytimes.com/2008/11/19/opinion/19romney.html?_r=2.
57. Center for Automotive Research, "The Impact on the U.S. Economy of the Successful Automaker Bankruptcies," CAR research memorandum, Nov. 17, 2010, http://www.cargroup.org/assets/files/bankruptcy.pdf.
58. Ibid.
59. http://www.treasury.gov/resource-center/data-chart-center/Documents/20120413_FinancialCrisisResponse.pdf.
60. http://www.nytimes.com/2011/11/30/business/center-for-automotive-research-predicts-sharp-gain-in-auto-jobs.html.
61. Robert Schoenberger, "Barack Obama, Democrats Call the Auto Bailouts a Success, but Did They Work?," *The Plain Dealer*, June 2, 2011, http://www.cleveland.com/business/index.ssf/2011/06/barack_obama_democrats_call_the_auto_bailouts_a_success_but_did_they_work.html.
62. Rich Klein, "President Obama Affirms His Support for Same Sex Marriage," ABC News, May 9, 2012, http://gma.yahoo.com/blogs/abc-blogs/president-obama-affirms-his-support-for-same-sex-marriage.html.
63. Gallup Poll, "Six in 10 Say Obama Same-Sex Marriage View Won't Sway Vote," May 11, 2012, http://www.gallup.com/poll/154628/six-say-obama-sex-marriage-view-won-sway-vote.aspx.
64. Nate Silver, "Support for Gay Marriage Outweighs Opposition in Polls," *New York Times*, May 9, 2012, http://fivethirtyeight.blogs.nytimes.com/2012/05/09/support-for-gay-marriage-outweighs-opposition-in-polls/.
65. Damla Ergun, "Strong Support for Gay Marriage Now Exceeds Strong Opposition," ABC News, May 23, 2012, http://abcnews.go.com/blogs/politics/2012/05/strong-support-for-gay-marriage-now-exceeds-strong-opposition.
66. Maggie Haberman, "Bush '04 pollster: Change in Attitudes on Gay Marriage Across the Board," *Politico*, May 11, 2012, http://www.politico.com/blogs/burns-haberman/2012/05/bush-pollster-change-in-attitudes-on-gay-marriage-123235.html.
67. President Barack Obama, "Remarks at the Signing of the Dodd-Frank Wall Street Reform and Consumer Protection Act," July 21, 2010, the White House Press Office, http://www.whitehouse.gov/the-press-office/remarks-president-signing-dodd-frank-wall-street-reform-and-consumer-protection-act.

68 White House, "Wall Street Reform," http://www.whitehouse.gov/wallstreetreform.
69 The Volcker Rule separates proprietary trading from banking; it prohibits banks from owning, investing, or sponsoring hedge funds, private equity funds, or proprietary trading operations for the bank's own profit.
70 President Barack Obama, "Remarks by the President on the Passage of Financial Regulatory Reform," July 15, 2010, the White House Press Office, http://www.whitehouse.gov/the-press-office/remarks-president-passage-financial-regulatory-reform.
71 Planned Parenthood press release, "Survey: Nearly Three in Four Voters in America Support Fully Covering Prescription Birth Control," October 12, 2010, http://www.plannedparenthood.org/about-us/newsroom/press-releases/survey-nearly-three-four-voters-america-support-fully-covering-prescription-birth-control-33863.htm.
72 National Business Group on Health, "Investing in Maternal and Child Health," 2007, http://www.businessgrouphealth.org/healthtopics/maternalchild/investing/docs/mch_toolkit.pdf.
73 "Keep America's Women Moving Forward: The Key to an Economy Built to Last," the White House Council on Women and Girls, April 2012, http://www.whitehouse.gov/sites/default/files/email-files/womens_report_final_for_print.pdf.
74 "Investing in Pell Grants to Make College Affordable," the White House, http://www.whitehouse.gov/issues/education/higher-education/investing-in-pell-grants-to-make-college-affordable.
75 "Health Care and Education Reconciliation Act of 2010," *FinAid.org*, http://www.finaid.org/educators/20100330hcera.phtml.
76 American Council on Education, "Summary of Education Provisions in Health Care and Education Reconciliation Act of 2010," http://www.acenet.edu/AM/Template.cfm?Section=Home&TEMPLATE=/CM/ContentDisplay.cfm&CONTENTID=36034.
77 "The Obameter: Promise Kept: Reform No Child Left Behind," *PolitiFact.com*, http://www.politifact.com/truth-o-meter/promises/obameter/promise/245/reform-no-child-left-behind/.
78 Richard Pérez-Peña, "District Grant Contest Unveiled," *New York Times*, May 22, 2012, http://www.nytimes.com/2012/05/22/education/us-school-districts-can-enter-race-to-top-competition.html.
79 Jennifer Epstein, "President Obama's report card on education policy," *Politico.com*, June 10, 2012, http://www.politico.com/news/stories/0612/77252.html.
80 President Barack Obama, speech at the University of Miami, February 23, 2012, http://www.PolitiFact.com/florida/statements/2012/mar/01/barack-obama/obama-says-us-has-record-number-oil-rigs-operating.
81 U.S. Energy Information Administration, "How Dependent is the US on Foreign Oil?," April 13, 2012, http://205.254.135.7/tools/faqs/faq.cfm?id=32&t=6.
82 Gus Lubin, "As Soon as Next Year, America Could Become the World's Leading Energy Producer," *Business Insider*, March 21, 2012, http://articles.businessinsider.com/2012-03-21/markets/31218775_1_citi-saudi-arabia-production.
83 Jim Snyder and Katarzyna Klimasinska, "Obama Pushes Natural-Gas Fracking to Create 600,000 Jobs," *Bloomberg Businessweek*, Jan. 29, 2012, http://www.businessweek.com/news/2012-01-29/obama-pushes-natural-gas-fracking-to-create-600-000-jobs.html.
84 White House, "The Blueprint for A Secure Energy Future: Progress Report," March 2012; http://www.whitehouse.gov/sites/default/files/email-files/the_blueprint_for_a_secure_energy_future_oneyear_progress_report.pdf.
85 Julie Percha, "Obama Says Safe Nuclear Power Plants Are a Necessary Investment," ABC News, Feb. 16, 2010, http://abcnews.go.com/blogs/politics/2010/02/obama-says-safe-nuclear-power-plants-are-a-necessary-investment.
86 White House, *The Blueprint for a Secure Energy Fugure: Progress Report*, March 2012, http://www.whitehouse.gov/sites/default/files/email-files/the_blueprint_for_a_secure_energy_future_oneyear_progress_report.pdf
87 Tom Cohen, "Obama Pledges Support for Veterans, Families," CNN, May 28, 2010, http://politicalticker.blogs.cnn.com/2012/05/28/obama-pledges-support-for-veterans-families.
88 White House Office of Management and Budget, "U.S. Department of Veterans Affairs: The Federal Budget, Fiscal Year 2012," http://www.whitehouse.gov/omb/factsheet_department_veterans.
89 Some sources for this information: http://www.benefits.va.gov/VOW/; http://www.whitehouse.gov/omb/factsheet_department_veterans; http://articles.cnn.com/2010-07-12/politics/veterans.ptsd_1_ptsd-michael-walcoff-post-traumatic-stress-disorder?_s=PM:POLITICS; http://vetlawyers.com/vetblog/index.php/2012/04/va-hopes-technology-modernization-will-speed-up-claims-process/; http://voices.

washingtonpost.com/federal-eye/2010/05/obama_signs_bill_expanding_hea.html; http://www.gpo.gov/fdsys/pkg/PLAW-111publ163/html/PLAW-111publ163.htm; http://www.epaperflip.com/aglaia/viewer.aspx?docid=1dc1e97f82884912a8932a3502c37c02.

90 Peter Baker, "Obama Begins Commemoration of Vietnam Era," *New York Times*, May 28, 2012, http://www.nytimes.com/2012/05/29/us/politics/obama-begins-commemoration-of-vietnam-era.html.

91 David Stout, "Senate Passes Bill to Restrict Credit Card Practices," *New York Times*, May 19, 2009, http://www.nytimes.com/2009/05/20/us/politics/20web-credit.html.

92 White House, "Fact Sheet: Reforms To Protect American Credit Card Holders," May 22, 2009, http://www.whitehouse.gov/the_press_office/Fact-Sheet-Reforms-to-Protect-American-Credit-Card-Holders.

93 The OCC study shows that as a result of the CARD Act, interest rate hikes on existing accounts have been dramatically curtailed. Prior to the CARD Act, approximately 15 percent of accounts were repriced over the course of a year; today that number is under 2 percent. The OCC study also shows that the CARD Act has substantially curbed late fees. The total amount of late fees paid by consumers dropped by more than half, from $901 million in January 2010 (before the effective date of the new late fee rules) to $427 million in November 2010 (the latest month for which data are available). Overlimit fees, according to the OCC study, have virtually disappeared in the credit card industry. The number of accounts charged an overlimit fee dropped from approximately 12 percent per year to about 1 percent. "CARD Act Factsheet," Consumer Finance Protection Bureau, March 22, 2011,http://www.consumerfinance.gov/credit-cards/credit-card-act/feb2011-factsheet.

94 Press release, Center for Medicare and Medicaid Services, "Over 5.2 Million People with Medicare Save $3.7 Billion on Prescription Drugs Thanks to Affordable Care Act," June 25, 2012, http://www.cms.gov/apps/media/press/release.asp?Counter=4388&intNumPerPage=10&checkDate=&srchType=1&numDays=3500&srchOpt=0&srchData=&keywordType=All&chkNewsType=1%2C+2%2C+3%2C+4%2C+5&intPage=&showAll=&pYear=&year=&desc=&cboOrder=date.

95 Janet Novack, "Medicare Premiums Rise Less Than Expected; Surcharges For Wealthy Fall", *Forbes*, Oct. 27, 2011; http://www.forbes.com/sites/janetnovack/2011/10/27/medicare-premiums-rise-less-than-expected-surcharges-for-wealthy-to-fall/

96 Alex Wayne, "Health Law Repeal to Cost Seniors $20,000, Fidelity Says," *Bloomberg.com*, May 9, 2012, http://www.bloomberg.com/news/2012-05-09/health-law-repeal-to-cost-seniors-20-000-fidelity-says.html.

97 Floyd Norris, "What Stocks and GDP Say About Obama's Chances," *New York Times*, March 23, 2012, http://www.nytimes.com/2012/03/24/business/economy/election-insight-from-the-stock-market-and-gdp.html.

98 Steven Rusolillo, "The Stock Market Loves Obama," the *Wall Street Journal*, Jan. 23, 2012, http://blogs.wsj.com/marketbeat/2012/01/23/the-stock-market-loves-president-obama.

99 Bob Drummond, "Stocks Return More with Democrats in White House: BGOV Barometer," Bloomberg, Feb. 22, 2012, http://www.bloomberg.com/news/2012-02-22/stocks-return-more-with-dem-in-white-house-bgov-barometer.html.

100 President Barack Obama, State of the Union Address, January 25, 2011, http://www.whitehouse.gov/the-press-office/2011/01/25/remarks-president-state-union-address.

101 President Barack Obama, speech at National Association of Latino Elected and Appointed Officials' Annual Conference, June 22, 2012, http://www.whitehouse.gov/photos-and-video/video/2012/06/22/president-obama-speaks-naleo-annual-conference#transcript.

102 True: "Obama says border patrol has doubled number of agents," PolitiFact Truth-O-Meter, May 10, 2011; http://www.PolitiFact.com.com/truth-o-meter/statements/2011/may/10/barack-obama/obama-says-border-patrol-has-doubled-number-agents/.

103 President Barack Obama, State of the Union Address, Janurary 24, 2012, http://www.whitehouse.gov/the-press-office/2012/01/24/remarks-president-state-union-address.

104 As of June 2012, more than six times as many as President Bush: "The Year of the Drone," Counterterrorism Strategy Initiative, June 26, 2012, http://counterterrorism.newamerica.net/drones.

105 President Barack Obama, "Weekly Address: It's Time for Congress to Act to Help Responsible Homeowners," White House, February 4, 2012, http://www.whitehouse.gov/the-press-office/2012/02/04/weekly-address-it-s-time-congress-act-help-responsible-homeowners.

106 U.S. Department of the Treasury, "Making Home Affordable: Program Progress Report Through 2012," April 2012, http://www.treasury.gov/initiatives/financial-stability/results/MHA-Reports/Documents/April%202012%20MHA%20Report%20WITH%20SERVICER%20ASSESSMENTS_FINAL.pdf.

107 Ibid.

108. Binyamin Appelbaum, "After Years of False Hopes, Signs of a Turn in Housing," *New York Times*, June 27, 2012, http://www.nytimes.com/2012/06/28/business/economy/new-indications-housing-recovery-is-under-way.html?hpw.

109. National Association of Realtors, "Pending Home Sales Up in May, Continue Pattern of Strong Annual Gains," June 27, 2012, http://www.realtor.org/news-releases/2012/06/pending-home-sales-up-in-may-continue-pattern-of-strong-annual-gains.

110. Board of Governors of the Federal Reserve, "Flow of the Funding of the United States: Flows and Outstandings First Quarter 2012," Federal Reserve statistical release, June 7, 2012, http://www.federalreserve.gov/releases/z1/Current/z1.pdf.

111. Justin Yurkanin, "Five questions with Mitt Romney," *Las Vegas Review-Journal*, October 17, 2012, http://www.lvrj.com/multimedia/Five-questions-with-Mitt-Romney-132028338.html.

112. Cardiff Garcia, "The Obama budget," *Financial Times*, February 13, 2012, http://ftalphaville.ft.com/blog/2012/02/13/879141/the-obama-budget/.

113. Charles Riley, "Obama's Budget: Where It Cuts," *CNN Money*, February 13, 2012, http://money.cnn.com/2012/02/13/news/economy/obama_budget_cuts/index.htm.

114. Rick Ungar, "Who Is the Smallest Government Spender Since Eisenhower? Would You Believe It's Barack Obama?," May 24, 2012, http://www.forbes.com/sites/rickungar/2012/05/24/who-is-the-smallest-government-spender-since-eisenhower-would-you-believe-its-barack-obama/.

115. http://www.whitehouse.gov/photos-and-video/video/2012/04/06/president-obama-speaks-white-house-forum-women-and-economy#transcript.

116. Mitt and Ann Romney, interview with Diane Sawyer, April 16, 2012, ABC News, transcript, http://abcnews.go.com/Politics/transcript-diane-sawyer-sits-mitt-ann-romney/story?id=16150624&singlePage=true#.T-PWsRem_kU.

117. Adam Liptak, "Court Under Roberts Is Most Conservative in Decades," *New York Times*, July 24, 2010, http://www.nytimes.com/2010/07/25/us/25roberts.html?pagewanted=all.

118. "Health Care Reform and the Supreme Court (Affordable Care Act)," June 29, 2012, http://topics.nytimes.com/top/reference/timestopics/organizations/s/supreme_court/affordable_care_act/index.html.

119. Tom Joyce, "Obama Talks About York: We Got Five Minutes to Ask Obama Your Questions." *York (PA) Sunday News*, March 30, 2008., http://nl.newsbank.com/nl-search/we/Archives?p_action=doc&p_docid=.

120. With apologies to Virginia O'Hanlon and the *New York Sun*. Given the current state of Virginia politics, only a half apology is due to my home state for any confusion.

121. Foon Rhee, "Obama Highlights Science Education," *Boston Globe*, Nov. 23, 2009, http://www.boston.com/news/politics/politicalintelligence/2009/11/obama_highlight_4.html.

122. Press release, "President Obama Launches 'Educate to Innovate' Campaign for Excellence in Science, Technology, Engineering & Math (Stem) Education," White House, November 23, 2009, http://www.whitehouse.gov/the-press-office/president-obama-launches-educate-innovate-campaign-excellence-science-technology-en.

123. "Republican Primary Candidates on Climate Change," *San Francisco Chronicle*, Feb. 5, 2012, http://www.sfgate.com/opinion/article/Republican-primary-candidates-on-climate-change-3000298.php.

124. "Mostly True: Mitt Romney's views on climate change have changed, says DNC," PolitiFact.com, November 28, 2011, http://www.politifact.com/truth-o-meter/statements/2011/nov/30/democratic-national-committee/mitt-romneys-views-climate-change-have-changed-say/.

125. http://obama.3cdn.net/4465b108758abf7a42_a3jmvyfa5.pdf

126. Stephen Adams, "Human Stem Cell Therapy Works in Blind Patients in First Trial," *Telegraph*, Jan. 23, 2012, http://www.telegraph.co.uk/science/science-news/9033582/Human-stem-cell-therapy-works-in-blind-patients-in-first-trial.html.

127. U.S. Department of Health & Human Services, "NIH and the American Recovery and Reinvestment Act (ARRA)," http://recovery.nih.gov/.

128. President Barack Obama, statement by the President on the Don't Ask, Don't Tell Repeal Act of 2010, CNN, Dec. 18, 2010; http://whitehouse.blogs.cnn.com/2010/12/18/obama-and-dadt.

129. United States Government Accountability Office, *Personnel and Cost Data Associated with Implementing DOD's Homosexual Conduct Policy*, report to Representative Susan A. Davis (D-San Diego), January 2011, http://www.gao.gov/new.items/d11170.pdf.

130. Ibid.

131 For 2004–2009, according to the Government Accountability Office. Average cost per service member from 1994–2003 was $42,825, according to the Palm Center study *Financial Cost of Don't Ask, Don't Tell: How Much Does the Gay Ban Cost?*, Feb. 2006, http://www.palmcenter.org/files/active/0/2006-FebBlueRibbonFinalRpt.pdf.

132 United States Government Accountability Office, *Personnel and Cost Data Associated with Implementing DOD's Homosexual Conduct Policy*, report to Representative Susan A. Davis (D-San Diego), Jan. 2011, http://www.gao.gov/new.items/d11170.pdf.

133 Department of Defense, "DOD Announces Recruiting and Retention Numbers for Fiscal 2011," United States Department of Defense Release Number 201011, Oct. 24, 2011, http://www.rs.af.mil/recruiteronline/story.asp?id=123277087.

134 Department of Defense, *Report of the Comprehensive Review of the Issues Associated with a Repeal of "Don't Ask, Don't Tell,"* Nov. 30, 2010, pp. 119–29, http://www.defense.gov/home/features/2010/0610_dadt/DADTReport_FINAL_20101130(secure-hires).pdf.

135 Brian Montopoli, "Analysis: Romney tax plan strongly favors the rich," *CBSNews.comrch 2*, 2012, http://www.cbsnews.com/8301-503544_162-57389459-503544/analysis-romney-tax-plan-strongly-favors-the-rich/.

136 Greg Sargent, "Economists: Romney's idea wouldn't fix short-term crisis and could make things worse," *Washington Post*, June 7, 2012, http://www.washingtonpost.com/blogs/plum-line/post/economists-romneys-ideas-wouldnt-fix-short-term-crisis-and-could-make-things-worse/2012/06/07/gJQAHKUWLV_blog.html.

137 Tom Hamburger, "Romney's Bain Capital invested in companies that moved jobs overseas," *Washington Post*, June 21, 2012, http://www.washingtonpost.com/business/economy/romneys-bain-capital-invested-in-companies-that-moved-jobs-overseas/2012/06/21/gJQAsD9ptV_story.html.

138 Glenn Kessler, "Mitt Romney and 10,000 jobs: an untenable figure," *Washington Post*, January 10, 2012, http://www.washingtonpost.com/blogs/fact-checker/post/mitt-romney-and-100000-jobs-an-untenable-figure/2012/01/09/gIQAIoihmP_blog.html.

139 Robert Farley, "Romney's Job Record Is Best (or Worst)," June 8, 2012, http://factcheck.org/2012/06/romneys-jobs-record-is-best-or-worst/.

140 Bill Adair and Louis Jacobson, "PolitiFact's guide to Romney's flip-flops," PolitiFact, May 18, 2012, http://www.PolitiFact.com/truth-o-meter/article/2012/may/18/PolitiFact.coms-guide-mitt-romneys-flip-flops/.

141 "Mitt Romney Favorability Rating," *Huffpost Politics*, June 27, 2012, http://elections.huffingtonpost.com/pollster/mitt-romney-favorability.

142 Washington Post–ABC News Poll, *Washington Post*, May 20, 2012, http://www.washingtonpost.com/wp-srv/politics/polls/postabcpoll_20120520.html.

143 Campaign 2012, "CNN/ORC Poll," April 15, 2012, http://www.pollingreport.com/wh12.htm#Kaiser.

144 Mitt Romney, Interview with Soledad O'Brien on *Starting Point*, CNN, February 1, 2012, http://cnnpressroom.blogs.cnn.com/2012/02/01/mitt-romney-middle-income-americans-are-focus-not-very-poor/.

145 Mitt Romney, Interview with Matt Lauer, *Today Show*, NBC, January 11, 2012, http://politicalwire.com/archives/2012/01/11/income_inequality_should_be_talked_about_in_quiet_rooms.html.

146 "Romney said today he'll 'replace and supersede' a recently imposed Obama administration order that halts the deportation of some illegal immigrants brought to the USA as children," Catalina Camia, "Romney vows to 'replace' Obama's immigration order," *USA Today*, June 21, 2012, http://content.usatoday.com/communities/onpolitics/post/2012/06/mitt-romney-immigration-naleo-/1.

147 Judd Legum, "9 Reasons Why Mitt Romney Is More Right Wing Than George W. Bush," *Think Progress*, April 24, 2012, http://thinkprogress.org/election/2012/04/24/470541/mitt-romney-versus-george-bush/.

148 Judd Legum, "9 Reasons Why Mitt Romney Is More Right Wing than George W. Bush," *ThinkProgress.org*, April 24, 2012. http://thinkprogress.org/election/2012/04/24/470541/mitt-romney-versus-george-bush/.

149 Truth-O-Meter, "True: Barack Obama says Mitt Romney's tax plan gives millionaires an average tax cut of $250,000," *PolitiFact.org*, http://www.politifact.com/truth-o-meter/statements/2012/may/08/barack-obama/barack-obama-says-mitt-romneys-tax-plan-gives-mill./

150 "Oh, I would like to get rid of the campaign finance laws that were put in place. McCain-Feingold is a disaster; get rid of it. Let people make contributions they want to make to campaigns," Mitt Romney, during GOP presidential primary debate held by Fox News and the *Wall Street Journal*, January 17, 2012, http://

foxnewsinsider.com/2012/01/17/transcript-fox-news-channel-wall-street-journal-debate-in-south-carolina/.

151 Truth-O-Meter, "Half Flip, Flipometer: On Mitt Romney and whether humans are causing climate change," *PolitiFact.org*, October 27, 2011, http://www.politifact.com/truth-o-meter/statements/2012/may/15/mitt-romney/mitt-romney-and-whether-humans-are-causing-climate/.

152 "Romney: Russia is our number one geopolitical foe," CNN, March 26, 2012, http://cnnpressroom.blogs.cnn.com/2012/03/26/romney-russia-is-our-number-one-geopolitical-foe/.

153 "About PolitiFact," *Tampa Bay Times PolitiFact.com*, http://www.politifact.com/about/.

154 "The Obameter: Tracking Obama's Campaign Promises," PolitiFact, June 26, 2012, http://www.PolitiFact.com/truth-o-meter/promises/obameter/.

155 James Traub, "Foreign Affairs," *Washington Monthly*, Jan. 2012, http://www.washingtonmonthly.com/magazine/january_february_2012/features/foreign_affairs 034475.php.

156 Daniel Larison, "Romney's Foreign Policy Incompetence Should Be a Huge Liability, But It Doesn't Seem to Be One," *American Conservative*, June 18, 2012, http://www.theamericanconservative.com/larison/romneys-foreign-policy-incompetence-should-be-a-huge-liability-but-it-doesnt-seem-to-be-one.

157 Pat Garofalo, "RNC Spokeswoman: Republican Economic Platform Will Be the Bush Program, 'Just Updated,'" Think Progress, April 23, 2012, http://thinkprogress.org/economy/2012/04/23/469123/rnc-spokeswoman-republican-economic-platform-will-be-the-bush-program-just-updated.

158 President Barack Obama, speech at Cuyahoga Community College, June 14, 2012, the White House Press Office, http://www.whitehouse.gov/the-press-office/2012/06/14/remarks-president-economy-cleveland-oh.

159 David Roeder, "Geithner in Chicago: Obama 'Prevented' a Depression," *Post-Tribune*, April 4, 2012, http://posttrib.suntimes.com/business/11710197-420/geithner-in-chicago-obama-prevented-a-depression.html.

160 President Barack Obama, Nobel Lecture at Oslo City Hall, December 10, 2009, http://www.nobelprize.org/nobel_prizes/peace/laureates/2009/obama-lecture_en.html.

161 Micheline Maynard, "GM Is No. 1 in the World Again in Auto Sales," Forbes, January 1, 2012, http://www.forbes.com/sites/michelinemaynard/2012/01/19/gm-is-back-in-the-auto-sales-drivers-seat/.

162 Colleen Curtis, "President Obama Announces New Fuel Economy Standards," the White House Blog, July 29, 2011, http://www.whitehouse.gov/blog/2011/07/29/president-obama-announces-new-fuel-economy-standards.

163 Todd Spangler, "Report: Obama's Gas-Mileage Boost Will Save $69B a Year," *USA Today*, April 20, 2012, http://content.usatoday.com/communities/driveon/post/2012/04/report-obamas-gas-mileage-boost-will-save-69b-a-year/1#.T-i0Oxee7W9.

164 President Barqack Obama, speech in Kabul, Afghanistan, May 1, 2012, http://www.nytimes.com/2012/05/02/world/asia/text-obamas-speech-in-afghanistan.html?pagewanted=all.

165 Cheryl Pellerin, "Obama, Karzai Sign Partnership Agreement in Kabul," American Forces Press Service, U.S. Department of Defense, May 1, 2012; http://www.defense.gov/news/newsarticle.aspx?id=116160.

166 President Barack Obama, State of the Union address, "An America Built to Last," Jan. 24, 2012, http://articles.boston.com/2012-01-25/politics/30659081_1_fair-share-hard-work-american.

167 "Executive Order 13583—Establishing a Coordinated Government-wide Initiative to Promote Diversity and Inclusion in the Federal Workforce," Aug. 18, 2011, the White House Press Office, http://www.whitehouse.gov/the-press-office/2011/08/18/executive-order-establishing-coordinated-government-wide-initiative-prom.

168 David Jackson, "Obama in 1991, Promoting Diversity at Harvard," *USA Today*, Mar. 7, 2012, http://content.usatoday.com/communities/theoval/post/2012/03/obama-at-harvard-law-promoting-diversity/1#.T-PmIxem_kV.

169 James A. Barnes, "Obama's Team: The Face of Diversity," *National Journal*, June 20, 2009, http://www.nationaljournal.com/njmagazine/nj_20090620_3869.php.

170 John Schwartz, "For Obama, a Record on Diversity but Delays on Judicial Confirmations," *New York Times*, Aug. 6, 2011, http://www.nytimes.com/2011/08/07/us/politics/07courts.html?pagewanted=all.

171 U.S. Equal Employment Oppurtunity Commission, "Annual Report on the Federal Work Force: Fiscal Year 2009," Table 3, http://www.eeoc.gov/federal/reports/fsp2009/index.cfm#sectiond.

172 "People," Office of Personnel and Management, http://www.opm.gov/diversityandinclusion/people/index.aspx.

173 Nobel Prize Committee , "The Nobel Peace Prize for 2009," October 9, 2009, http://www.nobelprize.org/nobel_prizes/peace/laureates/2009/press.html.

174 White House, "The President Donates Nobel Prize Money to Charity," March 11, 2010, http://www.whitehouse.gov/the-press-office/president-donates-nobel-prize-money-charity.

175 "Was Joe Biden's Swear a Big Deal?," ABC World News with Diane Sawyer, March 24, 2010, http://abcnews.go.com/WN/joe-biden-swears-open-mic-gaffe-big-deal/story?id=10187880#.T-ui5Bem_kU.

176 Joel K. Goldstein, "Despite image as gaffe machine, Biden is a skilled VP," *MinnPost*, May 16, 2012, http://www.minnpost.com/community-voices/2012/05/despite-image-gaffe-machine-biden-skilled-vp.

177 Chris Cillizza and Aaron Blake, "*Washington Post*–ABC News Poll: The historic polling heights of Hillary Clinton," Washington Post, April 25, 2012, http://www.washingtonpost.com/blogs/the-fix/post/the-historic-polling-heights-of-hillary-clinton/2012/04/25/gIQA9LOYgT_blog.html.

178 Jeffery Jones, "Barack Obama, Hillary Clinton Again Top Most Admired List," Gallup Poll, December 27, 2011, http://www.gallup.com/poll/151790/barack-obama-hillary-clinton-again-top-admired-list.aspx.

179 Jill Dougherty, "Hillary Clinton makes history," CNN, June 28, 2012, http://security.blogs.cnn.com/2012/06/28/clinton-marks-milestone-in-latvia/.

180 U.S. House of Representatives, "Border Protection, Antiterrorism, and Illegal Immigration Control Act of 2005," H.R. 4437 109th Congress, 2005–2006, http://www.govtrack.us/congress/bills/109/hr4437.

181 Joseph E. Stiglitz and Linda J. Bilmes, "The true cost of the Iraq war: 3 trillion and beyond," *Washington Post*, September 5, 2010, http://www.washingtonpost.com/wp-yn/content/article/2010/09/03/AR2010090302200.html.

182 "Taxes, the Deficit and the Economy," New York Times, September 22, 2012. http://www.nytimes.com/2011/09/22/opinion/taxes-the-deficit-and-the-economy.html?_r=2.

183 President Barack Obama, Speech on Election Night, November 4, 2008, http://www.npr.org/templates/story/story.php?storyId=96624326.

184 Jeffrey M. Jones, "Michelle Obama Remains Popular in U.S.," Gallup Poll, May 30, 2012, http://www.gallup.com/poll/154952/Michelle-Obama-Remains-Popular.aspx?utm_source=google&utm_medium=rss&utm_campaign=syndication.

185 Alicia M. Cohn, "Michelle Obama would 'absolutely not' run for president," *The Hill*, April 26, 2012, http://thehill.com/blogs/blog-briefing-room/news/224033-michelle-obama-would-absolutely-not-run-for-president.

186 http://www.youtube.com/watch?v=j87k1j4CpOw.

187 David Maraniss, "President Obama's basketball love affair has roots in Hawaii high school team," Washington Post, June 9, 2012, http://www.washingtonpost.com/sports/president-obamas-basketball-love-affair-has-roots-in-hawaii-high-school-team/2012/06/09/gJQApU2mQV_story.html.

187 Ibid. obamas-basketball-love-affair-has-roots-in-hawaii-high-school-team/2012/06/09/gJQApU2mQV_story.html

188 Ibid.

189 http://www.youtube.com/watch?v=NQ5VK2wUZXE&feature=youtu.be.

190 "Obama on NBA lockout: 'We need our basketball', Sporting News, Oct. 12, 2011, http://aol.sportingnews.com/nba/feed/2010-10/nba-labor/story/obama-on-nba-lockout-we-need-our-basketball.

191 Mark Memmott, "Politics, basketball top skills on Obama team," USA Today, December 22, 2008, http://www.usatoday.com/news/washington/2008-12-16-obamahoops_N.htm.

192 Jonathan Lemire, "Malia, Sasha may be Obama's most important advisers," *Daily News*, May 13, 2012,http://articles.nydailynews.com/2012-05-13/news/31692410_1_president-obama-malia-female-voters.

193 "Transcript: Robin Roberts ABC News Interview With President Obama," *Good Morning America*, May 9, 2012; http://abcnews.go.com/Politics/transcript-robin-roberts-abc-news-interview-president-obama/story?id=16316043&page=3#.T-5dNhem_kU.

194 http://www.youtube.com/watch?v=y6uHR90Sq6k&feature=player_embedded#!

195 http://www.youtube.com/watch?v=y6uHR90Sq6k&feature=player_embedded#!

196 "President Obama Sings Al Green's 'Let's Stay Together,' Sales Jump 490%," *Huffington Post*, January 27, 2012, http://www.huffingtonpost.com/2012/01/27/president-obama-sings-al-green-lets-stay-together-sales-jump_n_1236428.html.

197 http://www.youtube.com/watch?v=qo8nLMCLT60&feature=player_embedded.

198 http://www.youtube.com/watch?v=ZcbG7wLWthE&feature=player_embedded.
199 http://www.youtube.com/watch?v=Vvorqcgcdtw&feature=related.
200 Nancy Benack, "Obama Sings 'Sweet Home Chicago' During Blues Concert at White House (VIDEO)," *Huffington Post*, February 22, 2012, http://www.huffingtonpost.com/2012/02/21/obama-sings-sweet-home-chicago_n_1292576.html.
201 http://www.youtube.com/watch?v=x1-JZ4NgyIM&feature=related.
202 http://www.youtube.com/watch?v=g8o-swR9U_k.
203 Press release, "Mitt Romney Wins Dentists' Smile Election," *The Wealthy Dentist*, February 3, 2008; http://thewealthydentist.com/pressreleases/051-best-presidential-election-candidates-smile-dentist-survey.htm.
204 Deborah Blum, "Face It!," *Psychology Today*, September 3. 2010; http://www.psychologytoday.com/articles/200909/face-it.
205 Alicia M. Cohn, "Cher compliments Obama's manners, 'beautiful smile,'" *The Hill*, June 7, 2012, http://thehill.com/blogs/twitter-room/other-news/231505-singer-cher-compliments-obamas-manners-smile/.
206 Phillip Rucker, "Mitt Romney's dog-on-the-car-roof story continues to be his critics' best friend," *Washington Post*, March 14, 2012, http://www.washingtonpost.com/mitt-romneys-dog-on-the-car-roof-story-still-proves-to-be-his-critics-best-friend/2012/03/14/gIQAp2LxCS_story.html.
207 Kristi Keck, "CNNPolitics: Whoomp, there he is? Obama look-alike in '90s music video," CNN.com, June 7, 2010, http://articles.cnn.com/2010-06-07/politics/obama.music.video_1_obama-presidency-music-video-gawker?_s=PM:POLITICS
208 John McWhorter, "Gosh, Golly, Gee," *New Republic*, June 8, 2012, http://www.tnr.com/article/politics/magazine/103945/romney-language-mcwhorter.
209 Susan Page, "History not kind to president during second term," *USA Today*, January 20, 2005, http://www.usatoday.com/news/washington/2005-01-20-history_x.htm,
210 Susan Page, "History not kind to president during second term," *USA Today*, January 20, 2005, http://www.usatoday.com/news/washington/2005-01-20-history_x.htm,
211 Colleen J. Shogan, "The Contemporary Presidency: The Sixth-Year Curse," *Presidential Studies Quarterly* 36 (2006): 89–101.
212 In response to the Republican overreach on impeachment, Clinton actually gained five seats in the House and stayed even in the Senate.
213 Lawrence Summers, "Romney's fiscal fantasy plan," *Washington Post*, April 26, 2012, http://www.washingtonpost.com/opinions/romneys-fiscal-fantasy-plan/2012/04/26/gIQAR44zjT_story.html.
214 Office of Management and Budget, Executive Office of the president of the United States, "Budget of the U.S. Golvernment Fiscal 2013," http://www.whitehouse.gov/sites/default/files/omb/budget/fy2013/assets/budget.pdf.
215 Stephen F. Hayes, "Risk-Averse Romney," *Weekly Standard*, April 2, 2012, http://www.weeklystandard.com/articles/risk-averse-romney_634427.html.
216 Steven Erlanger and Sheryl Gay Stolberg, "Surprise Nobel for Obama Stirs Praise and Doubts," *New York Times*, October 9, 2009, http://www.nytimes.com/2009/10/10/world/10nobel.html.
217 Brian Montopoli, "The 'Obama Effect'? Perceptions of U.S. Improve Abroad," CBS News, April 9, 2010, http://www.cbsnews.com/8301-503544_162-20002840-503544.html.
218 "World warming to US under Obama, BBC poll suggests," April 19, 2010, http://news.bbc.co.uk/2/hi/in_depth/8626041.stm.
219 Brian Montopoli, "Political Hotsheet: The 'Obama Effect'? Perceptions of U.S. Improve Abroad," *CBSNews.com*, April 9, 2010, http://www.cbsnews.com/8301-503544_162-20002840-503544.html.
220 Pew Research Center, "Global Opinion of Obama Slips, International Policies Faulted," June 13, 2012, http://www.pewglobal.org/2012/06/13/global-opinion-of-obama-slips-international-policies-faulted/.
221 Domenico Montanaro, "Powell to Romney on foreign policy: 'Come on, Mitt, think,'" MSNBC, May 23, 2012, http://firstread.msnbc.msn.com/_news/2012/05/23/11831419-powell-to-romney-on-foreign-policy-come-on-mitt-think?lite.
222 "Dmitry Medvedev says Mitt Romney comment 'smelled of Hollywood,'" *The Telegraph* (UK), July 8, 2012, http://www.telegraph.co.uk/news/worldnews/barackobama/9169275/Dmitry-Medvedev-says-Mitt-Romney-comment-smelled-of-Hollywood.html.

Dear Reader,

There's lots of ways to join the conversation and share your own reasons to vote for Barack Obama.

Visit www.52ReasonsToVoteForObama.com
or www.whitmanstrategies.com.

Like us on Facebook *52 Reasons To Vote For Obama*.

Follow us on Twitter @52ReasonsObama.

Email me at 52Reasons@whitmanstrategies.com.

I'd love to hear from you!

—Bernard Whitman